Now first, as I shut the door,
I was alone
In the new house, and the wind
Began to moan.

Old at once was the house,
And I was old;
My ears were teased with the dread
Of what was foretold.

Nights of storm, days of mist without end;
Sad days when the sun
Shone in vain: old griefs and griefs
Not yet begun.

All was foretold me; naught
Could I foresee;
But I learned how the wind would sound
After these things should be.

Edward Thomas

1878
1917

EDWARD
THOMAS
A MIRROR of ENGLAND

ELIANE WILSON

Calligraphy & Illustration
FREDERICK MARNS

Shepheard-Walwyn · London

First published in this format 1985 by
Shepheard-Walwyn (Publishers) Ltd,
Suite 34, 26 Charing Cross Road,
London WC2H 0DH

ISBN 0 85683 082 8

Printed in Great Britain by Henry Ling Ltd, Dorchester,
on Harrow Matt paper made by St Regis International Ltd
and supplied by Eros Paper Company Ltd.

to Myfanwy

Acknowledgements

We are most grateful to all those who have helped us with this book: Myfanwy Thomas for her kindness and her generosity, and for permission to use copyright material from *As It Was and World Without End* and *Time and Again* by Helen Thomas; Edward Eastaway Thomas for the loan of his uncle's walking stick; Sheila Rosenberg for advice and encouragement; Anne Mallinson and Alan Martin, Chairman and Hon. Secretary of the Edward Thomas Fellowship; Dr Stephen Gill and Lincoln College, Oxford; Connie Rye, Lady Coulson, Jane and Alastair Langlands, the Rev. Douglas Snelgar, David and Cynthia Lindup, Mrs L. Sykes and Mrs A. Hale for their hospitality and cheerful support in a variety of weathers.

We wish to thank Laurence Whistler for allowing us to reproduce as endpapers his memorial windows to Edward and Helen Thomas at Eastbury and Steep; Gervase Farjeon for permission to quote from *The Last Four Years* and *The Green Roads* by Eleanor Farjeon; the Literary Trustees of Walter de la Mare and the Society of Authors as their representative for permission to include extracts from Walter de la Mare's Foreword to the *Collected Poems* of Edward Thomas; the Estate of Robert Frost and the publishers Jonathan Cape Limited for permission to reproduce 'Iris by Night' from *The Poetry of Robert Frost* edited by Edward Connery Lathem.

The text of the poems is taken from *The Collected Poems of Edward Thomas* edited by R. George Thomas. The photograph of Edward Thomas is from an original in the possession of Myfanwy Thomas.

Contents

List of Illustrations

Description of Endpapers

The endpapers illustrate windows dedicated to Edward and Helen Thomas, engraved by Laurence Whistler whose description of them is below:

LEFT — A memorial (1971) to Edward and Helen Thomas in the parish church of Eastbury, near Lambourn in Berkshire. In this village Helen Thomas spent the last twelve years of a fifty-years' widowhood that dated from the battle of Arras in 1917. She is buried at the top of the churchyard, where a row of beeches was planted soon afterwards.

Between the trees, one in bud, one bare, formal hands of sunlight confer a blessing on their names. Their initials and dates are on the bark of the Spring tree: on the Winter tree steel helmet and Sam Browne belt hang from a branch, to recall that this poet of the English countryside found his gift in war-time and wrote his poems chiefly as a soldier. In the distance can be seen the sarsen stone on the slope of a hill near Petersfield, with its memorial plaque to the poet — the spire of Steep church — and the cottage at Hodson Bottom in Wiltshire where the couple had been happy; and in the background the mountains of his Welsh origin. Lines from his poems, chosen by the engraver, are written across the landscape seemingly at random, so as to suggest the jottings of a poet in a notebook — or his thoughts in front of landscapes that inspired him. The titles of Helen Thomas's two books about their marriage, *As It Was* and *World Without End*, are engraved at each side.

From *The Image on the Glass*, John Murray in association with The Cupid Press, 1975.

RIGHT — Two memorial windows (1978) to Edward Thomas in Steep Church near Petersfield, Hampshire. To the left is a green road across hills, such as the poet loved to follow on his solitary travels, bordered by yews and flowering may. His jacket, taken from an original, hangs on a branch, together with his pipe, and his stick beside it, as if awaiting his return. The farther landscape and sky are on the back of the glass, which is about three feet tall.

Edward Thomas

To the right is engraved one of his poems, and above it, in mist, 'the new house' itself on a hilltop above Steep, where he and his family were the first occupants. Below is a sequence of doors shut or opening, the last opening on a Flanders battlefield; from which something rises that turns into the sun, and then into the door-latch he has just closed behind him, in the poem.

From *Scenes and Signs on Glass*, The Cupid Press, 1985

We gratefully acknowledge the kind permission of Laurence Whistler to reproduce both his text and illustrations.

Edward Thomas

On the morning of Easter Monday 1917, Edward Thomas was killed by the blast of a shell in the battle of Arras. He was mourned as an essayist, as a bibliographer and as one of the foremost critics of his time. He had published thirty volumes of topography, biography and *belles-lettres*, compiled or introduced sixteen editions and anthologies, written over a million and a half words of review — yet his talent for poetry was known only to close friends.

Of the one hundred and forty-four poems he wrote during the last two and a half years of his life, Thomas was to see only a dozen in print, and those under the pseudonym of 'Edward Eastaway'. He was conscious of his reputation as a critic and did not want readers 'to be confined by what they knew or thought of him already'. Six were privately printed by his friend James Guthrie, founder of the Pear Tree Press, four in the quarterlies, *Form* and *Root and Branch* and two which Edward included as his own contribution in his anthology *This England*.

My introduction to this selection of some eighty of Edward Thomas's poems is not intended to be a critical study of his poetry. His wife Helen once said that to dissect poetry is like pulling apart the wings of a swallow in order to understand the miracle of flying. Edward Thomas had the rare gift of friendship, and I have borrowed at times the words of some of the poet's friends. These, in their eloquent simplicity, are moving and illuminating tributes to a poet who, after sixteen years as a writer of prose, years of frustration and self-doubt, found a new voice to release all his pent-up emotions and feelings, his thoughts and memories, and through the medium of verse found himself engrossed and conscious of a possible perfection as he never was in prose:

Out of us all
That make rhymes,
Will you choose
Sometimes —

Edward Thomas

As the winds use
A crack in a wall
Or a drain,
Their joy or their pain
To whistle through —
Choose me,
You English words? . . .

Let me sometimes dance
With you,
Or climb
Or stand perchance
In ecstasy,
Fixed and free
In a rhyme,
As poets do.

In 1913, the literary scene was alive with the poetry of a new generation intent on breaking with the Victorian tradition. Among them were Walter de la Mare, Ralph Hodgson, W.H. Davies, John Masefield, James Stephens, Harold Monro. The poetry centre in Bloomsbury, which was to become known in the literary world as the Harold Monro Poetry Bookshop, had officially opened. Its first book, *Georgian Poetry 1911-1912*, an anthology of the verse of some seventeen new poets, had met with such a success, that Wilfrid Gibson, Lascelles Abercrombie, John Drinkwater and Rupert Brooke, decided to print their own new verse in a quarterly, *New Numbers*, from their rural retreat near Dymock on the borders of Gloucestershire and Herefordshire. Also spending the summer months of 1914 in that beautiful orchard country, together with the Dymock poets, was the American poet Robert Frost who was joined in August by Edward Thomas. 'Do you remember the still summer evening', wrote Wilfrid Gibson in his poem 'The Golden Room', recalling the company of writers gathered in his house:

We talked and laughed, but for the most part listened
While Robert Frost kept on and on and on
In his slow New England fashion for our delight,

Holding us with shrewd turns and racy quips
And the rare twinkle of his grave blue eyes?
We sat there in the lamplight, while the day
Died from rose-latticed casements, and the plovers
Called over the low meadows, till the owls
Answered them from the elms, we sat and talked —
Now a quick flash from Abercrombie, now
A murmured dry half-heard aside from Thomas,
Now a clear laughing word from Brooke; and then
Again Frost's rich and ripe philosophy
That had the body and tang of good draught cider
And poured as clear a stream.

Edward Thomas and Robert Frost had met the year before at the St. George's in St. Martin's Lane, a London restaurant frequented by writers and artists where, regularly every Tuesday, Edward joined a small circle of friends. After years of neglect in his own country, Frost had come to England and found a publisher for his poetry. On reading Frost's first book, *A Boy's Will*, Thomas, who had by then attained a pre-eminent position as a critic of new verse, sensed a kindred spirit and asked Ralph Hodgson to arrange a meeting. It was to be the beginning of a deep and strong friendship; after Edward's death, Frost called him 'the only brother I ever had' and expressed all the magic of their friendship in his poem 'Iris by Night':

One misty evening, one another's guide,
We two were groping down a Malvern side
The last wet fields and dripping hedges home.
There came a moment of confusing lights,
Such as according to belief in Rome
Were seen of old at Memphis on the heights
Before the fragments of a former sun
Could concentrate anew and rise as one.
Light was a paste of pigment in our eyes.
And there was a moon and then a scene
So watery as to seem submarine;
In which we two stood saturated, drowned.

The clover-mingled rowan on the ground
Had taken all the water it could as dew,
And still the air was saturated too,
Its airy pressure turned to water weight.
Then a small rainbow like a trellis gate,
A very small moon-made prismatic bow,
Stood closely over us through which to go.
And then we were vouchsafed the miracle
That never yet to other two befell
And I alone of us have lived to tell.
A wonder! Bow and rainbow as it bent,
Instead of moving with us as we went
(To keep the pots of gold from being found),
It lifted from its dewy pediment
Its two mote-swimming many coloured ends
And gathered them together in a ring.
And we stood in it softly circled round
From all division time or foe can bring
In a relation of elected friends.

To Frost's second book published in May 1914, *North of Boston*, Thomas gave one of its finest reviews: 'This is one of the most revolutionary books of modern time, but one of the quietest and least aggressive. It speaks and it is poetry . . .' Later in life, when he had become famous and acclaimed, the American would never fail to acknowledge his debt to the English poet.

For Thomas, Robert Frost had become an inspiration. 'Between him and Edward*,' wrote Helen, 'a most wonderful friendship grew up. He believed in Edward and loved him, understanding as no other man had ever understood, his strange complex temperament. The influence of this man on Edward's intellectual life was profound, and to it alone of outside influences is to be attributed that final and fullest expression of himself which Edward found in poetry. There began during that holiday a kind of

* *As It Was* and *World Without End* were written by Helen with fictitious names for the characters. *As It Was* was not written for publication but to help Helen to recover — by writing the memories of her life with Edward — from a breakdown caused by the long-delayed shock of his death.

spiritual and intellectual fulfilment which was to culminate two years later in his death. In that short time, most of it spent in the army, Edward was to pour out in poetry all the splendid experience of sadness and beauty; and in his poems is expressed for ever the tender loveliness of the English country'.

Edward Thomas's physical and spiritual relationship with Nature had deep roots going back to his childhood. The eldest of six brothers, he was born in Lambeth on March the 3rd, 1878. Both his parents came from Wales, where Edward was to spend many holidays and for which his strength of feeling never diminished. His father, 'eloquent and confident', but a stern man who did not inspire affection, was a staff clerk at the Board of Trade; his ambition for his elder son to follow a career in the Civil Service was to be frustrated and lead eventually to conflict and animosity:

> I may come near loving you
> When you are dead
> And there is nothing to do
> And much to be said.
>
> To repent that day will be
> Impossible
> For you, and vain for me
> The truth to tell.

But there was a bond of great tenderness between Edward and his mother as he recalled in his fragment of autobiography, *The Childhood of Edward Thomas*. 'Her singing at fall of night, especially if we were alone together, soothed and fascinated me, as though it had been divine at once the mightiest and the softest sound in the world'. She was a shy and retiring woman from whom Edward inherited his handsome features and his often melancholic temperament:

> None ever was so fair
> As I thought you . . .

Like other boys, Edward went fishing, bird-nesting, collecting butterflies, fighting and exploring the still unspoilt commons of South London.

And he read — he had discovered Richard Jefferies and the last words of *The Amateur Poacher* had become to him 'a gospel, an incantation'. 'Let us go out of these narrow modern days, whose twelve hours have somehow become shortened, into the sunlight and the pure wind. A something that the ancients thought divine can be found, and felt there still.' Whilst spending a holiday in Wiltshire, he became close friends with a bushy-bearded, toothless, reformed old poacher called David Uzzell, 'Dad', whom he later immortalized in his poem 'Lob':

> An old man's face, by life and weather cut
> And coloured, — rough, brown, sweet as any nut . . .

The old man and his young companion became inseparable and all through that long summer led a life straight out of a page of Jefferies. When years later, in 1908, Thomas was commissioned to write a *Life of Richard Jefferies*, a book hailed as one of the classics in critical biography, he repaid his debt to a writer with whom he had identified so early and so strongly.

Edward had begun to write while still a pupil at St. Paul's School. He kept a diary, wrote essays on his country walks, modelling his style after Jefferies' and some were published by the time he was seventeen. They were shown to the established literary critic and gifted essayist James Ashcroft Noble, a man of great charm, *un homme de lettres par excellence*, who seeing great promise in Edward's writing, took him under his tutelage. He patiently criticized Thomas's work, advised him to keep writing his diary, helped him to get his essays published, lent him books and discussed Keats and Shelley with him.

It was of a portrait of Shelley 'in its sensitive and melancholic beauty' that Edward's striking face reminded Helen when she met him in her father's study; and James Ashcroft encouraged the friendship which soon grew between his daughter, whose impulsive and demonstrative nature Edward needed, and his shy young protégé. After Edward's death, Helen wrote of their life together 'a restless sea, tide in, tide out, calm and storm, despair and ecstasy; never still, never easy, but always vivid and moving wave upon wave a deep glorious sea . . .' They are moving memories, in their aching tenderness, of the friendship which became unconscious love, of the passionate relationship which survived years of hardship and poverty

and during which Helen, whose love and faith in Edward never wavered, held the family together.

They had married whilst Edward was still at Oxford, reading history. His first year, during which he worked for a scholarship and lived as a non-collegiate student, had been lonely. He was still writing, but was uncertain and confused. He needed a mentor, but Noble had died from tuberculosis shortly before Edward's first book, *The Woodland Life*, had been accepted by Blackwood, and Thomas had now fallen under the influence of the man whose essays had inspired the Aesthetic Movement, Walter Pater, the author of *The Renaissance* and *Appreciations*. As a result, his style had become deliberate and precious — and he knew it: 'Only when a word has become necessary to him can a man use it safely; if he try to impress words by force on a sudden occasion, they will either perish of his violence or betray him', he wrote later in 1913, in a book on Pater, having broken at last from his strong influence.

In Autumn 1898, Edward took up residence at Lincoln College and started to play an active role in university life. He rowed for his college, joined the literary society, the Davenant, where he delivered several papers, and indulged in his passion for English Literature. He bought leather-bound early editions, delighting in reading and re-reading loved texts on beautiful old paper. He became conscious that 'the gift of love of a writer' — as he wrote in *Richard Jefferies* — 'is his power of using words. Nothing is more mysterious than this power, along with the kindred powers of artist and musician. It is the supreme proof, above beauty, physical strength, intelligence, that a man or woman lives. Lighter than gossamer, words can entangle and hold fast all that is loveliest, and strongest, and fleetest, and most enduring, in heaven and earth. They are for the moment, perhaps, excelled by the might of policy or beauty, but only for the moment, and then all has passed away; but the words remain . . . they mark our utmost achievement in time. They outlive the life of which they seem the lightest emanation — the proud, the vigorous, the melodious words'.

But in the summer of 1900, Edward sat for his degree in a despondent mood. Tormented by indecision and sick with worry about the future and the financial responsibilities he was facing as a husband and already a father, he had worked badly, and the second-class degree he obtained was to him a bitter disappointment.

After a break with his father — Edward had contemptuously refused once more to try for a post in the Civil Service — he moved with Helen and their son Merfyn, first to a dingy flat in Earlsfield, a suburb of South London, later to Balham. Determined to live by his pen, he set out to look for work in a series of unsuccessful visits to literary editors where he met only with vague promises, condescension, rejection, and from which the shy, easily hurt and proud young writer came back home depressed, angry, and hating himself for his failure.

At last he was successful with the *Daily Chronicle*, whose literary editor, H. W. Nevinson, has left a description of their first meeting: 'When he first came to me, I thought to myself, "Yet another poet . . ." He was tall, absurdly thin, and a face of attractive distinction and ultra-refinement was sicklied over with nervous melancholy . . . Almost too shy to speak, he sat down proudly and asked if I could give him work. I enquired what work he could do, and he said: "None". At once recognizing my former self in him, I asked whether he would like some reviewing on any subject and on what. He replied that he knew nothing of any subject, and was quite sure he could not write, but certainly he did want work of some sort . . . Of course, he at once became one of my very best reviewers, and soon one of my closest friends. Shy and reserved of feelings he always remained; too self-distrustful till nearly the end'.

The Book Review of the *Daily Chronicle* was at that time the most authoritative literary page, but reviewing was poorly paid and Edward had to sell, one by one, the precious books he had extravagantly and with so much love bought in his student days at Oxford. It was also exhausting — at times he reviewed up to fifteen books in a week, and it left him with very little time to do his own creative writing; by 1910, he would have published only two slim volumes of his essays: *Horae Solitariae*, dedicated to Owen Edwards, his former Oxford Tutor, and *Rose Acre Papers*, dedicated to one of his closest confidants, the poet, Gordon Bottomley.

Oppressed by the squalor of their surroundings, and longing for the country, in Autumn 1901, Edward moved his family to Kent, where their second child, a daughter named Bronwen, 'the genius of smiles', was born the following year. There were to be many such moves in the life of Helen and Edward who, with a blind childlike faith, each time believed that a new home meant a new beginning.

By the summer of 1905, Edward was utterly exhausted. His reputation as a critic of verse and *belles-lettres* had grown, bringing with it requests from other papers for signed reviews, and he had accepted in 1903 the commission for a book on Oxford, undertaking to write sixty-thousand words in four months at the rate of thirty shillings a thousand. After handing in the ms., Edward wrote to an Oxford friend, Ian MacAlister: 'If I were not poor, I would burn it all and laugh at the publisher. It is neither good hackwork, nor good Edward Thomas. It will hurt me very much to see it in print . . . It has left me dried up, and I feel that I shall never do good, slow, leisurely work again . . .' But the following year, he accepted another such commission, and with the help of opium wrote *Beautiful Wales*. To smoke opium had been a fashionable thing to do in Oxford, but now he used it as an escape and also to keep him going. Prophetically he wrote to a friend: 'only a catastrophe or an improbable development can ever make calm or happiness possible for me.'

Seven years later, in 1912, in his fictional autobiography, *The Happy-Go-Lucky Morgans*, he would portray himself as he thought others would remember him: 'Mr Torrance . . . wrote what he was both reluctant and incompetent to write, at the request of a firm of publishers whose ambition was to have a bad, but nice-looking, book on everything and everybody, written by some young university man with private means, by some vegetarian spinster, or a doomed hack like Mr. Torrance, . . . His books are not the man. They are known only to students at the British Museum who get them out once and no more, for they discover hasty compilations, ill-arranged, inaccurate, and incomplete, and swollen to ridiculous size for the sake of gain. They contain not one mention of the house under the hill where he was born . . . it was one of his pains that seldom more than once or twice a year came the mood for doing what seemed to him the highest he could, namely write verses.'

Edward had moved to Hampshire in 1906; first to Berryfield Cottage, 'the most beautiful place we have ever lived in,' and three years later to the New House in Wick Green. The long, low house, full of heavy oak —

where in 1910 a third child, Myfanwy, was born, — had been built by a generous neighbour, Geoffrey Lupton. A disciple of William Morris and Ruskin, he put all his philosophy and superb craftsmanship in the building of the new house, which he now offered to Edward for whatever rent he could afford. But they never felt at ease in the new house, and once again moved, to the small Yew Tree Cottage, in the village of Steep. The children attended Bedales School whose curriculum was based on the teachings of William Morris, and to help with the fees, Helen taught in the kindergarten and took boarders in during the holidays.

Edward loved the beautiful countryside with its hangers of yew, ash and beech swaying with travellers' joy, and the deep mysterious coombes, homes of foxes and owls, clothed with beeches from which hung honeysuckle and clematis. They had curious names like Strawberry Hanger, Juniper Hanger, Farewell Hanger, Shoulder of Mutton hill, ancient names in which he delighted and through which he felt himself linked with earlier generations. He loved the earth he was treading — he was part of its continuity. At one with nature 'in the perfect hour of the green of the grass, so intense that it had an earthly light of its own in the sunless mist', Edward should have found peace and contentment, but he had physically and mentally driven himself to the limits of his strength. One day, he strode out of his house with a revolver in his pocket: 'Death was an idea tinged with poetry in his mind — a kingly thing which was once only at any man's call. After it came annihiliation. To escape from the difficulty of life, from the hopeless search for something that would make it possible for him to go on living like anybody else without questioning, he was eager to hide himself away in annihiliation . . .'

In the last twelve years, besides reviewing, Thomas had edited Dyer, Herbert, Marlowe, Jefferies, Cobbett and Borrow. He had written critical and biographical studies of *Richard Jefferies*, *Maurice Maeterlinck*, *Algernon Charles Swinburne*, *George Borrow*, *Lafcadio Hearns*, *Walter Pater*, and *Feminine Influence on the Poets*. There were also 'colour books' *Oxford*, *Beautiful Wales*, *The Heart of England*, *The South Country*, *Windsor Castle*, *The Isle of Wight*, *The Icknield Way*, and there were collections of *Celtic Stories* and *Norse Tales*, anthologies of folk songs and English verse and popular natural histories of birds, butterflies and flowers. And, in 'six weeks of unusual energy', in 1909 came some uncommissioned pieces, later published as *Rest and Unrest* and *Light and Twilight*. 'I believe he has taken the wrong path and is wandering lost in the vast wilderness. He is essentially a poet ...' wrote his friend W. H. Hudson. Thomas was yet to meet Robert Frost.

Life, however, was not all pressure and despondency. Although reviewing had brought him no real sense of achievement, he had 'discovered' new poets, and not a few owed him the first recognition of their verse: 'I have often wondered idly how I should meet the apparition of a new poet ... and now all that I can do is to help to lay a cloak of journalist's words over which he may walk a little more easily to his just fame,' he wrote when reviewing the poems of the Welsh-born W. H. Davies to whom, besides praise, he also gave practical help and the hospitality of his home. In the evening, over beer and tobacco, in front of the fire, 'Sweet William' as the children called him, would recount the story of his wanderings which he would soon set to paper in *The Autobiography of a Super-Tramp*.

There was also Walter de la Mare, whose poetry Thomas loved for the simplicity of its style and its sense of magic, and who, in his inspired Foreword to Thomas's *Collected Poems* published in 1920, gave an intuitive and moving portrait of Edward:

> His face was fair, long and rather narrow, and in its customary gravity wore an expression rather distant and detached. There was a glint of gold in his sun-baked hair. The eyes ... were of a clear dark blue ... the lips were finely lined and wide, the chin square. His shoes were to his stature; the hands that had cradled so many wild birds' eggs, and were familiar with every flower in the Southern counties, were powerful and bony; the gestures few; the frame vigorous ... His smile could be whimsical, stealthy, shy, ardent, mocking, or drily ironical ... His voice was low and gentle but musical, with a curious sweetness and hollowness when he sang his old Welsh songs to his children. I have never heard English used so fastidiously and yet so unaffectedly as in his talk. *Style* in talk, indeed is a rare charm; and it was his. You could listen to it for its own sake, just as for its style solely you can read a book. He must have thought like that; like that he felt. There were things and people, blind, callous, indifferent, veneered, destructive he hated, because he loved life, loved to talk about it, rare and racy, old and charactered. He might avoid, did avoid, what intimidated,

> chilled, or made him self-conscious; he never condescended. So children and the aged, the unfriended and the free were as natural and welcome to him as swallows under the eaves . . . What he gave to a friend in his company was not only himself, but that friend's self made infinitely less clumsy and shallow than usual, and at ease . . . Nobody in this world closely resembling him have I ever had the happiness to meet: others of his friends have said the same thing . . .

There were also moments of calm happiness when Edward was fishing, gardening, doing carpentry, carrying a child on his shoulders when they went on picnics, singing songs whilst bathing them in front of the fire. And there were his close friendships; with Ian McAlister, Gordon Bottomley, Jesse Berridge, the rector of Little Baddow, later canon of Chelmsford, a gentle and much-loved friend to Helen and her children, Harry Hooton, who had married a friend of Helen, and Eleanor Farjeon whom Edward met in the late Autumn 1912. Eleanor, who was to become a popular and well-known writer of children's stories, poems and plays, was thirty-one then, lively but shy, and 'only just emerging from a fantasy life' — which she preserved in her writings — 'into one of natural human relationships'.

She belonged to a group of brilliant young people holding advanced ideas on art and music, with a passion for Wagner and the *Ballets Russes*. Among them were the brothers Bax; Arnold, the composer, and Clifford who every year in his Elizabethan manor at Broughton Gifford 'loved to recreate the Periclean Golden Age with a group of gifted young men' recounts Eleanor. Although Edward was an unenthusiastic cricketer, he was persuaded to join in 'the Cricket Week' the high spot of their year. 'Sport, though the paramount object, was far from the only qualification for that Eleven; you need not be a Jessop, or a Rhodes, as long as you had wit or charm or intellect, love of music and poetry, an interest in chess and indiscreet paper-games, a speculative mind, an eloquent tongue to discourse, could score a boundary in dialectics, or stump a sophistry outside its crease; such delights ruled the grey-stone manor morning and night . . . In this gay company, Edward that summer stood hunched reluctantly (in the long field too) on a different village green every day, and every evening took part in the bout-rimés . . . and the symposia of talk far into the night . . .'

In Eleanor, Edward found a friend in whom he could confide, express his doubts and hopes, and it was not long before she fell in love with him: 'He counted on me for friendship' she wrote in her Foreword to *The Last Four Years*, the memoirs of her friendship with Edward Thomas, and 'I loved him with all my heart. He was far too penetrating not to know this, but only by two words, in one of his last letters from France, did he allow himself to show me that he knew.' Of her unspoken and undemanding love, only her brother Bertie, Helen, and one or two close friends, had her confidence. 'Edward trusted me never to give it to him. If I had, our friendship must have come to an end.'

They corresponded, often met in London, and Eleanor came to Steep. On fine days, Helen would pack a picnic and Edward would lead them to some special haunt he loved. The children adored her and after their first walk, horrified by her ignorance of wild flowers, Bronwen gathered a hundred of them, taught her their names, and set her a test.

To someone like Eleanor who 'couldn't tell a sycamore from an ash, and was apt to write of trees as temples of Pan . . . to walk with Edward in the country was to see, hear, smell and know it with fresh senses. He was as alert to what was happening in and on the earth and the air above it, as is an animal in the grass or a bird on a tree. Just as certain friends who share their thought with you will sharpen your thinking, he had the effect, when you took the road together, of quickening your seeing and hearing through his own keen eyes and ears. You would not walk that road again as you did before. You would know it in a new way . . .'

On one of her earlier visits to Steep, Edward gave Eleanor a copy of his exquisite essays *Light and Twilight*. After reading it, she asked him 'Haven't you ever written poetry, Edward?' 'Me?' he uttered with a short, self-scornful laugh. 'I couldn't write a poem to save my life'. Yet reviewing had not only given Thomas a profound knowledge of contemporary literature, but also a deep critical appreciation of literary style. He had identified what he disliked in the style of his contemporaries and altered his own. In his prose, Frost would now detect the similar natural cadence of the human voice that he was himself using in his poetry.

At the beginning of August 1914, after completing *A Literary Pilgrim*, Edward left for his long-awaited visit to Frost in Gloucestershire. They spent every day of that holiday together. Frost had read *In Pursuit of Spring* and, recognizing that it was full of poetry in prose form which did not declare itself, was telling Edward to write in verse form in exactly the same cadence. They spoke of poetry incessantly.

> The sun used to shine while we two walked
> Slowly together, paused and started
> Again, and sometimes mused, sometimes talked
> As either pleased, and cheerfully parted
>
> Each night. We never disagreed
> Which gate to rest on. The to be
> And the late past we gave small heed
> We turned from men or poetry
>
> To rumours of the war . . .

Frost sailed back to America six months later. 'We were together to the exclusion of every other person and interest all through 1914 — 1914 was our year. I never had, I never shall have another such year of friendship . . .' wrote the American poet.

Thomas was soon commissioned to write short essays on the public reaction to the declaration of war and people's feelings for their country. They were collected, after his death, in a volume called *The Last Sheaf*. The year after, he compiled an anthology, *This England*, the England of English writers like Walton, in whose *Compleat Angler*, Edward was 'touching the antiquity and sweetness of England — English fields, English people, English poetry, all together'. There could not have been anyone more gifted to compile such an anthology than Edward Thomas, whose love of England had been the main theme of his books. To him, two little things in early English history suggested England vividly: 'One is the very stunted hawthorn round which the Battle of Ashdown mainly clashed . . . the other, the hoar apple tree where Harold's host met the Conquerer near Hastings.'

War had intensified his feelings for England. He disliked the jingoism of the popular press and the 'explicitly patriotic', but something he felt had to be done before he 'could look again composedly at English landscape, at the elms and poplars about the houses, at the purple headed wood-betony with two pairs of leaves on a stiff stem, who stand sentinel among the grasses and bracken by hedge-side or wood's edge . . .' Shortly after he had enlisted in July 1915, Eleanor asked him what he was fighting for. Thomas stooped down, picked up a handful of earth, the English earth for which he was ready to give his life, and crumbling it through his fingers answered: 'Literally, for this.'

War also released the voice stilled within him for so many years. The demand for reviews and commissioned work had fallen (*The Life of The Duke of Marlborough* would be his last commission) and for the first time, Edward found himself with the freedom to write what he pleased. In December he began to write poetry. The depression which had tormented him so often ebbed away. Every day, he climbed the steep hanger up to the study which Lupton had generously let him continue to use, hardly able to contain the excitement in him. 'I am in it and no mistake' he wrote to Frost and sent him his first five poems. Frost's immediate response was enthusiastic. From then on, Edward wrote every day in a burst of intense creativity. By mid-February he had written some thirty poems. To Eleanor, to whom he was regularly sending his verses and which they discussed before she typed them, he wrote: 'I am trying to get rid of the last rags of rhetoric and formality which left my prose so often with a dead rhythm only'. His own fluency worried him. 'A man can't do all that and be any good . . .' but he had had sixteen years of apprenticeship with words and they had chosen him. He knew what he wished to avoid in his poetry and his self-awareness and self-criticism made him write with a remarkable maturity, and originality. The critics to whom he sent his poems failed at first to understand, disturbed by an individuality which did not comply with the formal techniques and the limited range of feelings of the typical Georgian poetry.

Having decided not to accept Frost's invitation to visit him in America, whilst the war was still on, Edward enlisted in the Artists' Rifles in July 1915. After two months in London, he was sent as a map-reading instructor at a camp in Essex, and in November 1916 was commissioned as an artillery officer.

He kept on writing poetry, scribbling verses in pencil on the backs of envelopes, on scraps of paper covered with gunnery calculations, and sent them all to Eleanor to type. In December, he volunteered for service in France and was given a short leave during which he said farewells to friends — they all sensed it was a final visit.

His last Christmas was spent at home and in January came the final parting from Helen whose love for him had never lost its passionate intensity. 'We cannot say why we love people' she wrote. 'There is no reason for passionate love. But the quality in him that I most admired was his sincerity. There was never any pretence between us. All was open and true. Often he was bitter and cruel, but I could bear it because I knew all. There was nothing left for me to guess at, no lies, no falsity. All was known, all was suffered and endured; and afterwards there was no reserve in our joy. If we love deeply we must also suffer deeply; for the price for the capacity for ecstatic joy is anguish. And so it was with us to the end.'

On the 29th of January, he left for France with Frost's new book of verse in his haversack. He volunteered for duty in the front-line and was sent to Arras, where the build-up for the Easter offensive was in progress. He got on well with the much younger men in his battery and became a father figure to them. 'Your husband was greatly loved,' wrote his captain to Helen,' and his going has been a personal loss to each of us . . . He was always the same, quietly cheerful, and ready to do any job that was going with the same steadfast unassuming spirit . . . I wish I could convey to you the picture of him, a picture we had all learnt to love, of the old clay pipe, gum boots, oilskin coat, and steel helmet . . .'

Edward wrote no more poems from the front, but kept up the war diary he had started on the first of January: 'Up at 5. worn out and wretched. 5.9s flopping on Achicourt while I dressed . . . Blackbirds in the clear cold bright morning early in black Beaurains. Sparrows in the elder of the hedge I observe through — a cherry tree just this side of hedge makes projection in trench with its roots. Beautiful clear evening everything dark and soft round Neuville Vitasse, after the rainbow there and the last shower. Night in lilac-bush cellar of stone like Berryfield. Letter to Helen. Machine gun bullets snaking along — hissing like little wormy serpents'.

He wrote letters home and also to Robert Frost who, back in America, had placed a few of Edward's poems with Harriet Monroe's *Poetry*, a Chicago magazine. 'I think I get surer of some primitive things that one has got to get sure of about oneself and other people, and I think less about return than I thought I should — partly no doubt I inhibit the idea of return. I only think by flashes of the things at home that I used to enjoy and should again . . . I doubt if anybody here thinks less of home than I do and yet I doubt if anybody loves it more . . .'

In March, *An Annual of New Poetry*, with eighteen of his poems appeared in England. Thomas never received the copy that Gordon Bottomley had hastened to send him, but he saw the review of the TLS which called Edward Eastaway 'a real poet, with the truth in him'.

On the ninth of April, the Battle of Arras began. 'When Edward Thomas was killed', wrote Walter de la Mare in his Foreword to the *Collected Poems* — and to whom I acknowledge my debt for the title of this book — 'a mirror of England was shattered of so pure and true a crystal that a clearer and tenderer reflection of it can be found no other where than in these poems . . .'

Edward Thomas was buried in the military cemetery of Agny, not far from where he fell. A bush of Old Man, the hoar-green feathery herb of the poem — which Robert Frost called 'the flower of the lot' — flourishes on his grave. It also flourishes at the foot of the Sarsen Memorial Stone erected to the poet's memory on the Shoulder of Mutton hill, in Hampshire, the source of inspiration of so many of his poems.

And I rose up and knew
That I was tired,
And continued my journey.

Eliane Wilson
Harrow on the Hill
January 1985

The Poems

Words

Out of us all
That make rhymes,
Will you choose
Sometimes—
As the winds use
A crack in a wall
Or a drain,
Their joy or their pain
To whistle through—
Choose me,
You English words?
I know you:
You are light as dreams,
Tough as oak,
Precious as gold,
As poppies and corn,
Or an old cloak:
Sweet as our birds
To the ear;

As the burnet rose
In the heat
Of Midsummer:
Strange as the races
Of dead and unborn:
Strange and sweet
Equally,
And familiar,
To the eye,
As the dearest faces
That a man knows,
And as lost homes are:
But though older far
Than oldest yew,—
As our hills are, old,—
Worn new
Again and again;
Young as our streams
After rain:
And as dear
As the earth which you prove
That we love.

Make me content
With some sweetness
From Wales
Whose nightingales
Have no wings,—
From Wiltshire and Kent
And Herefordshire,
And the villages there,—
From the names, and the things
No less.

Let me sometimes dance
With you,
Or climb
Or stand perchance
In ecstasy,
Fixed and free
In a rhyme,
As poets do.

I took one or two steps to the stile and, in-
stead of crossing it I leaned upon the gate at
one side. The confidence and ease deepen-
ed and darkened as if I also were like that
still, sombre cloud that had been a copse,
under the pale sky that was light without shed-
ding light. I did not disturb the dark rest
and beauty of the earth which had ceased to
be ponderous, hard matter and had become
itself cloudy or, as it is when the mind thinks
of it, spiritual stuff, so that the glow-worms
shone through it as stars through clouds. I
found myself running without weariness or
heaviness of the limbs through the soaked
overhanging grass. I knew that I was more
than the something which had been looking
out all that day upon the visible earth and
thinking and speaking and tasting friend-
ship. Somewhere—close at hand in that rosy
thicket or far off beyond the ribs of sunset
—I was gathered up with an immortal com-

pany, where I and poet and lover and flower and cloud and star were equals, as all the little leaves were equal ruffling before the gusts, or sleeping and carved out of the silentness. And in that company I had learned that I am something which no fortune can touch, whether I be soon to die or long years away. Things will happen which will trample and pierce, but I shall go on, something that is here and there like the wind, something unconquerable, something not to be separated from the dark earth and the light sky, a strong citizen of infinity and eternity. The confidence and ease had become a deep joy; I knew that I could not do without the Infinite, nor the Infinite without me.

Light and Twilight

The Signpost

The dim sea glints chill. The white sun is shy,
And the skeleton weeds and the never-dry,
Rough, long grasses keep white with frost
At the hilltop by the finger-post;
The smoke of traveller's-joy is puffed
Over hawthorn berry and hazel tuft.

I read the sign. Which way shall I go?
A voice says: You would not have doubted so
At twenty. Another voice gentle with scorn
Says: At twenty you wished you had never been born.

One hazel lost a leaf of gold
From a tuft at the tip, when the first voice told
The other he wished to know what 'twould be

To be sixty by this same post.' You shall see'
He laughed – and I had to join his laughter –
'You shall see; but either before or after,
Whatever happens, it must befall,
A mouthful of earth to remedy all
Regrets and wishes shall freely be given;
And if there be a flaw in that heaven
'Twill be freedom to wish, and your wish may be
To be here or anywhere talking to me,
No matter what the weather, on earth,
At any age between death and birth,
To see what day or night can be,
The sun and the frost, the land and the sea,
Summer, Autumn, Winter, Spring,
With a poor man of any sort, down to a king,
Standing upright out in the air
Wondering where he shall journey, O where?'

The Other

The forest ended. Glad I was
To feel the light, and hear the hum
Of bees, and smell the drying grass
And the sweet mint, because I had come

To an end of forest, and because
Here was both road and inn, the sum
Of what's not forest. But 'twas here
They asked me if I did not pass
Yesterday this way? 'Not you? Queer.'
'Who then? and slept here?' I felt fear.

I learnt his road and, ere they were
Sure I was I, left the dark wood
Behind, kestrel and woodpecker,
The inn in the sun, the happy mood
When first I tasted sunlight there.
I travelled fast, in hopes I should
Outrun that other. What to do
When caught, I planned not. I pursued
To prove the likeness, and, if true,
To watch until myself I knew.

I tried the inns that evening
Of a long gabled high-street grey,
Of courts and outskirts, travelling
An eager but a weary way,
In vain. He was not there. Nothing
Told me that ever till that day
Had one like me entered those doors,
Save once. That time I dared: 'You may
Recall'—but never-foamless shores
Make better friends than those dull boors.

Many and many a day like this
Aimed at the unseen moving goal
And nothing found but remedies
For all desire. These made not whole;
They sowed a new desire, to kiss
Desire's self beyond control,
Desire of desire. And yet
Life stayed on within my soul.
One night in sheltering from the wet
I quite forgot I could forget.

A customer, then the landlady
Stared at me. With a kind of smile
They hesitated awkwardly:
Their silence gave me time for guile.
Had anyone called there like me,
I asked. It was quite plain the wile
Succeeded. For they poured out all.
And that was naught. Less than a mile
Beyond the inn, I could recall
He was like me in general.

He had pleased them, but I less.
I was more eager than before
To find him out and to confess,
To bore him and to let him bore.
I could not wait: children might guess
I had a purpose, something more
That made an answer indiscreet.
One girl's caution made me sore,
Too indignant even to greet
That other had we chanced to meet.

I sought then in solitude.
The wind had fallen with the night; as still
The roads lay as the ploughland rude,
Dark and naked, on the hill.
Had there been ever any feud
'Twixt earth and sky, a mighty will
Closed it: the crocketed dark trees,
A dark house, dark impossible
Cloud-towers, one star, one lamp, one peace
Held on an everlasting lease:

And all was earth's, or all was sky's;
No difference endured between
The two. A dog barked on a hidden rise;
A marshbird whistled high unseen;
The latest waking blackbird's cries
Perished upon the silence keen.

The last light filled a narrow firth
Among the clouds. I stood serene,
And with a solemn quiet mirth,
An old inhabitant of earth.

Once the name I gave to hours
Like this was melancholy, when
It was not happiness and powers
Coming like exiles home again,
And weakness quitting their bowers,
Smiled and enjoyed, far off from men,
Moments of everlastingness.
And fortunate my search was then
While what I sought, nevertheless,
That I was seeking, I did not guess.

That time was brief: once more at inn
And upon road I sought my man
Till once amid a tap-room's din
Loudly he asked for me, began
To speak, as if it had been a sin,
Of how I thought and dreamed and ran
After him thus, day after day:
He lived as one under a ban
For this: what had I got to say?
I said nothing. I slipped away.

And now I dare not follow after
Too close. I try to keep in sight,
Dreading his frown and worse his laughter.
I steal out of the wood to light;
I see the swift shoot from the rafter
By the inn door: ere I alight
I wait and hear the starlings wheeze
And nibble like ducks: I wait his flight.
He goes: I follow: no release
Until he ceases. Then I also shall cease.

Melancholy

The rain and wind, the rain and wind, raved endlessly.
On me the Summer storm, and fever, and melancholy
Wrought magic, so that if I feared the solitude
Far more I feared all company: too sharp, too rude,

Had been the wisest or the dearest human voice.
What I desired I knew not, but whate'er my choice
Vain it must be, I knew. Yet naught did my despair
But sweeten the strange sweetness, while through the wild air
All day long I heard a distant cuckoo calling
And, soft as dulcimers, sounds of near water falling,
And, softer, and remote as if in history,
Rumours of what had touched my friends, my foes, or me.

Digging 1

Today I think
Only with scents,– scents dead leaves yield,
And bracken, and wild carrot's seed,
And the square mustard field;

Odours that rise
When the spade wounds the roots of tree,
Rose, currant, raspberry, or goutweed,
Rhubarb or celery;

The smoke's smell, too,
Flowing from where a bonfire burns
The dead, the waste, the dangerous,
And all to sweetness turns.

It is enough
To smell, to crumble the dark earth,
While the robin sings over again
Sad songs of Autumn mirth.

Aspens

All day and night, save winter, every weather,
Above the inn, the smithy, and the shop,
The aspens at the cross-roads talk together
Of rain, until their last leaves fall from the top.

Out of the blacksmith's cavern comes the ringing
Of hammer, shoe, and anvil; out of the inn
The clink, the hum, the roar, the random singing—
The sounds that for these fifty years have been.

The whisper of the aspens is not drowned,
And over lightless pane and footless road,
Empty as sky, with every other sound
Not ceasing, calls their ghosts from their abode,

A silent smithy, a silent inn, nor fails
In the bare moonlight or the thick-furred gloom,
In tempest or the night of nightingales,
To turn the cross-roads to a ghostly room.

And it would be the same were no house near.
Over all sorts of weather, men, and times,
Aspens must shake their leaves and men may hear
But need not listen, more than to my rhymes.

Whatever wind blows, while they and I have leaves
We cannot other than an aspen be
That ceaselessly, unreasonably grieves,
Or so men think who like a different tree.

Old Man

Old Man, or Lad's-love,– in the name there's nothing
To one that knows not Lad's-love, or Old Man,
The hoar-green feathery herb, almost a tree,
Growing with rosemary and lavender.
Even to one that knows it well, the names
Half decorate, half perplex, the thing it is:
At least, what that is clings not to the names
In spite of time. And yet I like the names.

The herb itself I like not, but for certain
I love it, as some day the child will love it
Who plucks a feather from the door-side bush
Whenever she goes in or out of the house.
Often she waits there, snipping the tips and shrivelling
The shreds at last on to the path, perhaps

Thinking, perhaps of nothing, till she sniffs
Her fingers and runs off. The bush is still
But half as tall as she, though it is as old;
So well she clips it. Not a word she says;
And I can only wonder how much hereafter–

She will remember, with that bitter scent,
Of garden rows, and ancient damson-trees
Topping a hedge, a bent path to a door,
A low thick bush beside the door, and me
Forbidding her to pick.

As for myself,
Where first I met the bitter scent is lost.
I, too, often shrivel the grey shreds,
Sniff them and think and sniff again and try
Once more to think what it is I am remembering,
Always in vain. I cannot like the scent,
Yet I would rather give up others more sweet,
With no meaning, than this bitter one.

I have mislaid the key. I sniff the spray
And think of nothing; I see and I hear nothing;
Yet seem, too, to be listening, lying in wait
For what I should, yet never can, remember:
No garden appears, no path, no hoar-green bush
Of Lad's-love, or Old Man, no child beside,
Neither father nor mother, nor any playmate;
Only an avenue, dark, nameless, without end.

Beauty

What does it mean? Tired, angry, and ill at ease,
No man, woman, or child, alive could please
Me now. And yet I almost dare to laugh
Because I sit and frame an epitaph–
'Here lies all that no one loved of him
And that loved no one.' Then in a trice that whim
Has wearied. But, though I am like a river
At fall of evening while it seems that never
Has the sun lighted it or warmed it, while
Cross breezes cut the surface to a file,
This heart, some fraction of me, happily
Floats through the window even now to a tree
Down in the misting, dim-lit, quiet vale,
Not like a pewit that returns to wail
For something it has lost, but like a dove
That slants unswerving to its home and love.
There I find my rest, as through the dusk air
Flies what yet lives in me: Beauty is there.

The Word

There are so many things I have forgot,
That once were much to me, or that were not,
All lost, as is a childless woman's child
And its child's children, in the undefiled
Abyss of what can never be again.
I have forgot, too, names of the mighty men
That fought and lost or won in the old wars,
Of kings and fiends and gods, and most of the stars.
Some things I have forgot that I forget.
But lesser things there are, remembered yet,
Than all the others. One name that I have not—
Though 'tis an empty thingless name—forgot
Never can die because Spring after Spring
Some thrushes learn to say it as they sing.
There is always one at midday saying it clear
And tart—the name, only the name I hear.
While perhaps I am thinking of the elder scent
That is like food, or while I am content
With the wild rose scent that is like memory,
This name suddenly is cried out to me
From somewhere in the bushes by a bird
Over and over again, a pure thrush word.

The Glory

The glory of the beauty of the morning,—
The cuckoo crying over the untouched dew;
The blackbird that has found it, and the dove
That tempts me on to something sweeter than love;
White clouds ranged even and fair as new-mown hay;
The heat, the stir, the sublime vacancy
Of sky and meadow and forest and my own heart:—
The glory invites me, yet it leaves me scorning
All I can ever do, all I can be,
Beside the lovely of motion, shape, and hue,
The happiness I fancy fit to dwell
In beauty's presence. Shall I now this day
Begin to seek as far as heaven, as hell,
Wisdom or strength to match this beauty, start

And tread the pale dust pitted with small dark drops,
In hope to find whatever it is I seek,
Hearkening to short-lived happy-seeming things
That we know naught of, in the hazel copse?
Or must I be content with discontent
As larks and swallows are perhaps with wings?
And shall I ask at the day's end once more
What beauty is, and what I can have meant
By happiness? And shall I let all go,
Glad, weary, or both? Or shall I perhaps know
That I was happy oft and oft before,
Awhile forgetting how I am fast pent,
How dreary-swift, with naught to travel to,
Is Time? I cannot bite the day to the core.

The Ash Grove

Half of the grove stood dead, and those that yet lived made
Little more than the dead ones made of shade.
If they led to a house, long before they had seen its fall:
But they welcomed me; I was glad without cause and delayed.

Scarce a hundred paces under the trees was the interval—
Paces each sweeter than sweetest miles—but nothing at all,
Not even the spirits of memory and fear with restless wing,
Could climb down in to molest me over the wall

That I passed through at either end without noticing.
And now an ash grove far from those hills can bring
The same tranquillity in which I wander a ghost
With a ghostly gladness, as if I heard a girl sing

The song of the Ash Grove soft as love uncrossed,
And then in a crowd or in distance it were lost,
But the moment unveiled something unwilling to die
And I had what most I desired, without search or desert or cost.

The Bridge

I have come a long way today:
On a strange bridge alone,
Remembering friends, old friends,
I rest, without smile or moan,
As they remember me without smile or moan.

All are behind, the kind
And the unkind too, no more
Tonight than a dream. The stream
Runs softly yet drowns the Past,
The dark-lit stream has drowned the Future and the Past.

No traveller has rest more blest
Than this moment brief between
Two lives, when the Night's first lights
And shades hide what has never been,
Things goodlier, lovelier, dearer, than will be or have been.

I never saw that land before

I never saw that land before,
And now can never see it again;
Yet, as if by acquaintance hoar
Endeared, by gladness and by pain,
Great was the affection that I bore

To the valley and the river small,
The cattle, the grass, the bare ash trees,
The chickens from the farmsteads, all
Elm-hidden, and the tributaries
Descending at equal interval;

The blackthorns down along the brook
With wounds yellow as crocuses
Where yesterday the labourer's hook
Had sliced them cleanly; and the breeze
That hinted all and nothing spoke.

I neither expected anything
Nor yet remembered: but some goal
I touched then; and if I could sing
What would not even whisper my soul
As I went on my journeying,

I should use, as the trees and birds did,
A language not to be betrayed;
And what was hid should still be hid
Excepting from those like me made
Who answer when such whispers bid.

He is fortunate who can find an ideal England of the past, the present and the future to worship, and embody it in his native fields, and waters or his garden, as in a graven image.

.....Going up such a road, between steep banks of chalk and the roots and projecting bases of beeches whose foliage meets overhead—a road worn twenty feet deep, and now scarce ever used as a footpath except by fox and hare—we may be half-conscious that we have climbed that way before during the furrowing of the road, and we move as in a dream between this age and that dim one which we vainly strive to recover.

But because we are imperfectly versed in history, we are not therefore blind to the past. The eye that sees the things of to-day, and the ear that hears, the mind that contemplates or dreams, is itself an instrument of an antiquity equal to whatever it is called upon to apprehend. We are not merely twentieth-century Londoners or Kentish men or Welshmen. We belong to the days of Wordsworth, of Elizabeth, of Richard Plantagenet, of Harold, of the earliest bards. We, too, like Taliesin, have borne a banner before Alexander, have been with our Lord in the manger of the ass, have been in India, and with the "remnant of Troia", and with Noah in the ark, and our original country is "the region of the summer stars." And of these many folds in our nature the face of the earth reminds us, and perhaps, even where there are no more marks visible upon the land than there were in Eden, we are aware of the passing of time in ways too difficult and strange for the explanation of historian and zoologist and philosopher. It is this manifold nature that responds with such indescribable depth and variety to the appeals of many landscapes.

The South Country

Lob

At hawthorn-time in Wiltshire travelling
In search of something chance would never bring,
An old man's face, by life and weather cut
And coloured,– rough, brown, sweet as any nut,–
A land face, sea-blue-eyed,– hung in mind
When I had left him many a mile behind.
All he said was: 'Nobody can't stop 'ee. It's
A footpath, right enough. You see those bits
Of mounds – that's where they opened up the barrows
Sixty years since, while I was scaring sparrows.
They thought as there was something to find there,
But couldn't find it, by digging, anywhere.'

To turn back then and seek him, where was the use?
There were three Manningfords,– Abbots, Bohun, and Bruce:
And whether Alton, not Manningford, it was
My memory could not decide, because
There was both Alton Barnes and Alton Priors.

All had their churches, graveyards, farms, and byres,
Lurking to one side up the paths and lanes,
Seldom well seen except by aeroplanes;
And when bells rang, or pigs squealed, or cocks crowed,
Then only heard. Ages ago the road
Approached. The people stood and looked and turned,
Nor asked it to come nearer, nor yet learned
To move out there and dwell in all men's dust.
And yet withal they shot the weathercock, just
Because 'twas he crowed out of tune, they said:
So now the copper weathercock is dead.
If they had reaped their dandelions and sold
Them fairly, they could have afforded gold.

Many years passed, and I went back again
Among those villages, and I looked for men
Who might have known my ancient. He himself
Had long been dead or laid upon the shelf,
I thought. One man I asked about him roared
At my description: "'Tis old Bottlesford
He means, Bill.' But another said: 'Of course,
It was Jack Button up the White Horse.

He's dead, sir, these three years.' This lasted till
A girl proposed Walker of Walker's Hill,
'Old Adam Walker. Adam's Point you'll see
Marked on the maps.'

'That was her roguery'
The next man said. He was a squire's son
Who loved wild bird and beast, and dog and gun
For killing them. He had loved them from his birth,
One with another, as he loved the earth.
'The man may be like Button, or Walker, or
Like Bottlesford, that you want, but far more
He sounds like one I saw when I was a child.
I could almost swear to him. The man was wild
And wandered. His home was where he was free.
Everybody has met one such man as he.
Does he keep clear old paths that no one uses
But once a life-time when he loves or muses?
He is English as this gate, these flowers, this mire.
And when at eight years old Lob-lie-by-the-fire
Came in my books, this was the man I saw.
He has been in England as long as dove and daw,
Calling the wild cherry tree the merry tree,
The rose campion Bridget-in-her-bravery;

And in a tender mood he, as I guess,
Christened one flower Live-in-idleness,
And while he walked from Exeter to Leeds
One April called all cuckoo-flowers Milkmaids.
From him old herbal Gerard learnt, as a boy,
To name wild clematis the Traveller's-joy.

Our blackbirds sang no English till his ear
Told him they called his Jan Toy "Pretty dear."
(She was Jan Toy the Lucky, who, having lost
A shilling, and found a penny loaf, rejoiced.)
For reasons of his own to him the wren
Is Jenny Pooter. Before all other men
'Twas he first called the Hog's Back the Hog's Back.
That Mother Dunch's Buttocks should not lack
Their name was his care. He too could explain
Totteridge and Totterdown and Juggler's Lane:
He knows, if anyone. Why Tumbling Bay,
Inland in Kent, is called so, he might say.

'But little he says compared with what he does.
If ever a sage troubles he will buzz
Like a beehive to conclude the tedious fray:
And the sage, who knows all languages, runs away.
Yet Lob has thirteen hundred names for a fool,
And though he never could spare time for school
To unteach what the fox so well expressed,
On biting the cock's head off,– Quietness is best,–
He can talk quite as well as anyone
After his thinking is forgot and done.
He first of all told someone else's wife,
For a farthing she'd skin a flint and spoil a knife
Worth sixpence skinning it. She heard him speak:
"She had a face as long as a wet week"
Said he, telling the tale in after years.
With blue smock and with gold rings in his ears,
Sometimes he is a pedlar, not too poor
To keep his wit. This is tall Tom that bore
The logs in, and with Shakespeare in the hall
Once talked, when icicles hung by the wall.
As Herne the Hunter he has known hard times.

On sleepless nights he made up weather rhymes
Which others spoilt. And, Hob being then his name,
He kept the hog that thought the butcher came
To bring his breakfast. "You thought wrong" said Hob.
When there were kings in Kent this very Lob,
Whose sheep grew fat and he himself grew merry,
Wedded the king's daughter of Canterbury;
For he alone, unlike squire, lord, and king,
Watched a night by her without slumbering;
He kept both waking. When he was but a lad
He won a rich man's heiress, deaf, dumb, and sad,
By rousing her to laugh at him. He carried
His donkey on his back. So they were married.
And while he was a little cobbler's boy
He tricked the giant coming to destroy
Shrewsbury by flood. "And how far is it yet?"
The giant asked in passing. "I forget;
But see these shoes I've worn out on the road
And we're not there yet." He emptied out his load
Of shoes. The giant sighed, and dropped from his spade
The earth for damming Severn, and thus made
The Wrekin hill; and little Ercall hill
Rose where the giant scraped his boots. While still
So young, our Jack was chief of Gotham's sages.

But long before he could have been wise, ages
Earlier than this, while he grew thick and strong
And ate his bacon, or, at times, sang a song
And merely smelt it, as Jack the giant-killer
He made a name. He, too, ground up the miller,
The Yorkshireman who ground men's bones for flour.

'Do you believe Jack dead before his hour?
Or that his name is Walker, or Bottlesford,
Or Button, a mere clown, or squire, or lord?
The man you saw,—Lob-lie-by-the-fire, Jack Cade,
Jack Smith, Jack Moon, poor Jack of every trade,
Young Jack, or old Jack, or Jack What-d'ye-call,
Jack-in-the-hedge, or Robin-run-by-the-wall,
Robin Hood, Ragged Robin, lazy Bob,
One of the lords of No Man's Land, good Lob,—
Although he was seen dying at Waterloo,
Hastings, Agincourt, and Sedgmoor, too,—
Lives yet. He never will admit he is dead
Till millers cease to grind men's bones for bread,

Not till our weathercock crows once again
And I remove my house out of the lane
On to the road.' With this he disappeared
In hazel and thorn tangled with old-man's-beard.
But one glimpse of his back, as there he stood,
Choosing his way, proved him of old Jack's blood,
Young Jack perhaps, and now a Wiltshireman
As he has oft been since his days began.

The Manor Farm

The rock-like mud unfroze a little and rills
Ran and sparkled down each side of the road
Under the catkins wagging in the hedge.
But earth would have her sleep out, spite of the sun;
Nor did I value that thin gilding beam
More than a pretty February thing
Till I came down to the old Manor Farm,
And church and yew-tree opposite, in age
Its equals and in size. Small church, great yew,
And farmhouse slept in a Sunday silentness.
The air raised not a straw. The steep farm roof,
With tiles duskily glowing, entertained
The midday sun; and up and down the roof
White pigeons nestled. There was no sound but one.
Three cart-horses were looking over a gate
Drowsily through their forelocks, swishing their tails
Against a fly, a solitary fly.

The Winter's cheek flushed as if he had drained
Spring, Summer, and Autumn at a draught
And smiled quietly. But 'twas not Winter—
Rather a season of bliss unchangeable
Awakened from farm and church where it had lain
Safe under tile and thatch for ages since
This England, Old already, was called Merry.

But these things also

But these things also are Spring's—
On banks by the roadside the grass
Long-dead that is greyer now
Than all the Winter it was;

The shell of a little snail bleached
In the grass; chip of flint, and mite
Of chalk; and the small birds' dung
In splashes of purest white:

All the white things a man mistakes
For earliest violets
Who seeks through Winter's ruins
Something to pay Winter's debts,

While the North blows, and starling flocks
By chattering on and on
Keep their spirits up in the mist,
And Spring's here, Winter's not gone.

March

Now I know that Spring will come again,
Perhaps tomorrow: however late I've patience
After this night following on such a day.

While still my temples ached from the cold burning
Of hail and wind, and still the primroses
Torn by the hail were covered up in it,
The sun filled earth and heaven with a great light
And a tenderness, almost warmth, where the hail dripped,
As if the mighty sun wept tears of joy.
But 'twas too late for warmth. The sunset piled
Mountains on mountains of snow and ice in the west:
Somewhere among their folds the wind was lost,
And yet 'twas cold, and though I knew that Spring
Would come again, I knew it had not come,
That it was lost, too, in those mountains cold.

What did the thrushes know? Rain, snow, sleet, hail,
Had kept them quiet as the primroses.
They had but an hour to sing. On boughs they sang,
On gates, on ground; they sang while they changed perches
And while they fought, if they remembered to fight:
So earnest were they to pack into that hour
Their unwilling hoard of song before the moon
Grew brighter than the clouds. Then 'twas no time
For singing merely. So they could keep off silence
And night, they cared not what they sang or screamed,
Whether 'twas hoarse or sweet or fierce or soft,
And to me all was sweet: they could do no wrong.
Something they knew—I also, while they sang
And after. Not till night had half its stars
And never a cloud, was I aware of silence
Rich with all that riot of songs, a silence
Saying that Spring returns, perhaps tomorrow.

Tall Nettles

Tall nettles cover up, as they have done
These many springs, the rusty harrow, the plough
Long worn out, and the roller made of stone:
Only the elm butt tops the nettles now.

This corner of the farmyard I like most:
As well as any bloom upon a flower
I like the dust on the nettles, never lost
Except to prove the sweetness of a shower.

The Wind's Song

Dull-thoughted, walking among the nunneries
Of many a myriad anemones
In the close copses, I grew weary of Spring
Till I emerged and in my wandering
I climbed the down up to a lone pine clump
Of six, the tallest dead, one a mere stump.
On one long stem, branchless and flayed and prone
I sat in the sun listening to the wind alone,
Thinking there could be no old song so sad
As the wind's song; but later none so glad
Could I remember as that same wind's song
All the time blowing the pine boughs among.
My heart that had been still as the dead tree
Awakened by the West wind was made free.

Sedge-Warblers

This beauty makes me dream there was a time
Long past and irrecoverable, a clime
Where river of such radiance racing clear
Through buttercup and kingcup bright as brass
But gentle, nourishing the meadowgrass
That leans and scurries in the wind, would bear
Another beauty, divine and feminine,
Child of the sun, whose happy soul unstained
Could love all day, and never hate or tire,
Lover of mortal or immortal kin.

And yet rid of this dream, ere I had drained
Its poison, quieted was my desire
So that I only looked into the water
And hearkened, while it combed the dark-green hair
And shook the millions of the blossoms white
Of water crowfoot, and curdled in one sheet
The flowers fallen from the chestnuts in the park

Far off. The sedgewarblers that hung so light
On willow twigs, sang longer than any lark,
Quick, shrill or grating, a song to match the heat
Of the strong sun, nor less the water's cool
Gushing through narrows, swirling in the pool.

Their song that lacks all words, all melody,
All sweetness almost, was dearer now to me
Than sweetest voice that sings in tune sweet words:
This was the best of May, the small brown birds
Wisely reiterating endlessly
What no man learnt yet, in or out of school.

The Pond

Bright clouds of may
Shade half the pond.
Beyond,
All but one bay
Of emerald
Tall reeds
Like criss-cross bayonets
Where a bird once called,
Lies bright as the sun.
No one heeds.
The light wind frets
And drifts the scum
Of may-blossom.
Till the moorhen calls
Again
Naught's to be done
By birds or men.
Still the may falls.

Sowing

It was a perfect day
For sowing: just
As sweet and dry was the ground
As tobacco-dust.

I tasted deep the hour
Between the far
Owl's chuckling first soft cry
And the first star.

A long stretched hour it was;
Nothing undone
Remained; the early seeds
All safely sown.

And now, hark at the rain,
Windless and light,
Half a kiss, half a tear,
Saying good-night.

Haymaking

After night's thunder far away had rolled
The fiery day had a kernel sweet of cold,
And in the perfect blue the clouds uncurled,
Like the first gods before they made the world
And misery, swimming the stormless sea
In beauty and in divine gaiety.
The smooth white empty road was lightly strewn
With leaves – the holly's Autumn falls in June –
And fir cones standing stiff up in the heat.
The mill-foot water tumbled white and lit
With tossing crystals, happier than any crowd
Of children pouring out of school aloud.

And in the little thickets where a sleeper
For ever might lie lost, the nettle-creeper
And garden warbler sang unceasingly;
While over them shrill shrieked in his fierce glee
The swift with wings and tail as sharp and narrow
As if the bow had flown off with the arrow.
Only the scent of woodbine and hay new-mown
Travelled the road. In the field sloping down,
Park-like, to where its willows showed the brook,
Haymakers rested. The tosser lay forsook
Out in the sun; and the long waggon stood
Without its team; it seemed it never would
Move from the shadow of that single yew.

The team, as still, until their task was due,
Beside the labourers enjoyed the shade
That three squat oaks mid-field together made
Upon a circle of grass and weed uncut,
And on the hollow, once a chalk-pit, but
Now brimmed with nut and elder-flower so clean.
The men leaned on their rakes, about to begin,
But still. And all were silent. All was old,
This morning time, with a great age untold,
Older than Clare and Cowper, Morland and Crome,
Than, at the field's far edge, the farmer's home,
A white house crouched at the foot of a great tree.
Under the heavens that know not what years be
The men, the beasts, the trees, the implements
Uttered even what they will in times far hence—
All of us gone out of the reach of change—
Immortal in a picture of an old grange.

Adlestrop

Yes, I remember Adlestrop—
The name, because one afternoon
Of heat the express-train drew up there
Unwontedly. It was late June.

The steam hissed. Someone cleared his throat.
No one left and no one came
On the bare platform. What I saw
Was Adlestrop—only the name

And willows, willow-herb, and grass,
And meadowsweet, and haycocks dry,
No whit less still and lonely fair
Than the high cloudlets in the sky.

And for that minute a blackbird sang
Close by, and round him, mistier,
Farther and farther, all the birds
Of Oxfordshire and Gloucestershire.

October

The green elm with the one great bough of gold
Lets leaves into the grass slip, one by one. –
The short hill grass, the mushrooms small milk-white,
Harebell and scabious and tormentil,
That blackberry and gorse, in dew and sun,
Bow down to; and the wind travels too light
To shake the fallen birch leaves from the fern;
The gossamers wander at their own will.
At heavier steps than birds' the squirrels scold.

The late year has grown fresh again and new
As Spring, and to the touch is not more cool
Than it is warm to the gaze; and now I might
As happy be as earth is beautiful,
Were I some other or with earth could turn
In alternation of violet and rose,
Harebell and snowdrop, at their season due,
And gorse that has no time not to be gay.
But if this be not happiness, who knows?
Some day I shall think this a happy day,
And this mood by the name of melancholy
Shall no more blackened and obscured be.

There's nothing like the sun

There's nothing like the sun as the year dies,
Kind as it can be, this world being made so,
To stones and men and beasts and birds and flies,
To all things that it touches except snow,
Whether on mountain side or street of town.
The south wall warms me: November has begun,
Yet never shone the sun as fair as now
While the sweet last-left damsons from the bough
With spangles of the morning's storm drop down
Because the starling shakes it, whistling what
Once swallows sang. But I have not forgot
That there is nothing, too, like March's sun,
Like April's, or July's, or June's, or May's,
Or January's, or February's, great days:
And August, September, October, and December
Have equal days, all different from November.
No day of any month but I have said—
Or, if I could live long enough, should say—
'There's nothing like the sun that shines today.'
There's nothing like the sun till we are dead.

November Sky

November's days are thirty:
November's earth is dirty,
Those thirty days, from first to last;
And the prettiest things on ground are the paths
With morning and evening hobnails dinted,
With foot and wing-tip overprinted
Or separately charactered,
Of little beast and little bird.
The fields are mashed by sheep, the roads
Make the worst going, the best the woods
Where dead leaves upward and downward scatter.
Few care for the mixture of earth and water,
Twig, leaf, flint, thorn,
Straw, feather, all that men scorn,
Pounded up and sodden by flood,
Condemned as mud.

But of all the months when earth is greener
Not one has clean skies that are cleaner.
Clean and clear and sweet and cold,
They shine above the earth so old,
While the after-tempest cloud
Sails over in silence though winds are loud,
Till the full moon in the east
Looks at the planet in the west
And earth is silent as it is black,
Yet not unhappy for its lack.
Up from the dirty earth men stare:
One imagines a refuge there
Above the mud, in the pure bright
Of the cloudless heavenly light:
Another loves earth and November more dearly
Because without them, he sees clearly,
The sky would be nothing more to his eye
Than he, in any case, is to the sky;
He loves even the mud whose dyes
Renounce all brightness to the skies.

After Rain

The rain of a night and a day and a night
Stops at the light
Of this pale choked day. The peering sun
Sees what has been done.
The road under the trees has a border new
Of purple hue
Inside the border of bright thin grass:
For all that has
Been left by November of leaves is torn
From hazel and thorn
And the greater trees. Throughout the copse
No dead leaf drops

On grey grass, green moss, burnt-orange fern,
At the wind's return:
The leaflets out of the ash-tree shed
Are thinly spread
In the road, like little black fish, inlaid,
As if they played.
What hangs from the myriad branches down there
So hard and bare
Is twelve yellow apples lovely to see
On one crab-tree,
And on each twig of every tree in the dell
Uncountable
Crystals both dark and bright of the rain
That begins again.

The Combe

The Combe was ever dark, ancient and dark.
Its mouth is stopped with bramble, thorn, and briar;
And no one scrambles over the sliding chalk
By beech and yew and perishing juniper
Down the half precipices of its sides, with roots
And rabbit holes for steps. The sun of Winter,
The moon of Summer, and all the singing birds
Except the missel-thrush that loves juniper,
Are quite shut out. But far more ancient and dark
The Combe looks since they killed the badger there,
Dug him out and gave him to the hounds,
That most ancient Briton of English beasts.

Bronwen

If I should ever by chance grow rich
I'll buy Codham, Cockridden, and Childerditch,
Roses, Pyrgo, and Lapwater,
And let them all to my elder daughter.
The rent I shall ask of her will be only
Each year's first violets, white and lonely,
The first primroses and orchises—
She must find them before I do, that is.
But if she finds a blossom on furze
Without rent they shall all for ever be hers,
Codham, Cockridden, and Childerditch,
Roses, Pyrgo and Lapwater,—
I shall give them all to my elder daughter.

Merfyn

If I were to own this countryside
As far as a man in a day could ride,
And the Tyes were mine for giving or letting,–
Wingle Tye and Margaretting
Tye,– and Skreens, Gooshays, and Cockerells,
Shellow, Rochetts, Bandish, and Pickerells,
Martins, Lambkins, and Lillyputs,
Their copses, ponds, roads, and ruts,
Fields where plough-horses steam and plovers
Fling and whimper, hedges that lovers
Love, and orchards, shrubberies, walls
Where the sun untroubled by north wind falls,
And single trees where the thrush sings well
His proverbs untranslatable,
I would give them all to my son
If he would let me any one
For a song, a blackbird's song, at dawn.

He should have no more, till on my lawn
Never a one was left, because I
Had shot them to put them into a pie,—
His Essex blackbirds, every one,
And I was left old and alone.

Then unless I could pay, for rent, a song
As sweet as a blackbird's, and as long—
No more— he should have the house, not I:
Margaretting or Wingle Tye,
Or it might be Skreens, Gooshays, or Cockerells,
Shellow, Rochetts, Bandish, or Pickerells,
Martins, Lambkins, or Lillyputs,
Should be his till the cart tracks had no ruts.

Myfanwy

What shall I give my daughter the younger
More than will keep her from cold and hunger?
I shall not give her anything.
If she shared South Weald and Havering,
Their acres, the two brooks running between,
Paine's Brook and Weald Brook,
With pewit, woodpecker, swan, and rook,
She would be no richer than the queen
Who once on a time sat in Havering Bower
Alone, with the shadows, pleasure and power.
She could do no more with Samarcand,
Or the mountains of a mountain land
And its far white house above cottages
Like Venus above the Pleiades.
Her small hands I would not cumber
With so many acres and their lumber,
But leave her Steep and her own world
And her spectacled self with hair uncurled,
Wanting a thousand little things
That time without contentment brings.

Frederick Mains

Helen

And you, Helen, what should I give you?
So many things I would give you
Had I an infinite great store
Offered me and I stood before
To choose. I would give you youth,
All kinds of loveliness and truth,
A clear eye as good as mine,
Lands, waters, flowers, wine,
As many children as your heart
Might wish for, a far better art
Than mine can be, all you have lost
Upon the travelling waters tossed,
Or given to me. If I could choose
Freely in that great treasure-house
Anything from any shelf,
I would give you back yourself,
And power to discriminate
What you want and want it not too late,
Many fair days free from care
And heart to enjoy both foul and fair,
And myself, too, if I could find
Where it lay hidden and it proved kind.

Celandine

Thinking of her had saddened me at first,
Until I saw the sun on the celandines lie
Redoubled, and she stood up like a flame,
A living thing, not what before I nursed,
The shadow I was growing to love almost,
The phantom, not the creature with bright eye
That I had thought never to see, once lost.

She found the celandines of February
Always before us all. Her nature and name
Were like those flowers, and now immediately
For a short swift eternity back she came,
Beautiful, happy, simply as when she wore
Her brightest bloom among the winter hues
Of all the world; and I was happy too,
Seeing the blossoms and the maiden who
Had seen them with me Februarys before,
Bending to them as in and out she trod
And laughed, with locks sweeping the mossy sod.

But this was a dream: the flowers were not true,
Until I stooped to pluck from the grass there
One of five petals and I smelt the juice
Which made me sigh, remembering she was no more
Gone like a never perfectly recalled air.

It rains

It rains, and nothing stirs within the fence
Anywhere through the orchard's untrodden, dense
Forest of parsley. The great diamonds
Of rain on the grassblades there is none to break,
Or the fallen petals further down to shake.

And I am nearly as happy as possible
To search the wilderness in vain though well,
To think of two walking, kissing there,
Drenched, yet forgetting the kisses of the rain:
Sad, too, to think that never, never again,

Unless alone, so happy shall I walk
In the rain. When I turn away, on its fine stalk
Twilight has fined to naught, the parsley flower
Figures, suspended still and ghostly white,
The past hovering as it revisits the light.

Home 2

Often I had gone this way before:
But now it seemed I never could be
And never had been anywhere else;
'Twas home; one nationality
We had, I and the birds that sang,
One memory.

They welcomed me. I had come back
That eve somehow from somewhere far:
The April mist, the chill, the calm,
Meant the same thing familiar
And pleasant to us, and strange too,
Yet with no bar.

The thrush on the oak top in the lane
Sang his last song, or last but one;
And as he ended, on the elm
Another had but just begun
His last; they knew no more than I
The day was done.

Then past his dark white cottage front
A labourer went along, his tread
Slow, half with weariness half with ease;
And, through the silence, from his shed
The sound of sawing rounded all
That silence said.

For these (Prayer)

An acre of land between the shore and the hills,
Upon a ledge that shows my kingdoms three,
The lovely visible earth and sky and sea,
Where what the curlew needs not, the farmer tills:

A house that shall love me as I love it,
Well-hedged, and honoured by a few ash-trees
That linnets, greenfinches, and goldfinches
Shall often visit and make love in and flit:

A garden I need never go beyond,
Broken but neat, whose sunflowers every one
Are fit to be the sign of the Rising Sun:
A spring, a brook's bend, or at least a pond:

For these I ask not, but, neither too late
Nor yet too early, for what men call content,
And also that something may be sent
To be contented with, I ask of fate.

It was upon

It was upon a July evening.
At a stile I stood, looking along a path
Over the country by a second Spring
Drenched perfect green again. 'The lattermath
Will be a fine one.' So the stranger said,
A wandering man. Albeit I stood at rest
Flushed with desire I was. The earth outspread,
Like meadows of the future, I possessed.

And as an unaccomplished prophecy
The stranger's words, after the interval
Of a score years, when those fields are by me
Never to be recrossed, now I recall,
This July eve, and question, wondering,
What of the lattermath to this hoar Spring?

Then one evening the new moon made a difference. It was the end of a wet day; at least, it had begun wet, had turned warm and muggy, and at last fine but still cloudy. The sky was banded with rough masses in the north-west, but the moon, a stout orange crescent, hung free of cloud near the horizon. At one stroke, I thought, like many other people, what things that same new moon sees eastward about the Meuse in France. Of those who could see it there, not blinded by smoke, pain, or excitement, how many saw it and heeded? I was deluged, in a second stroke, by another thought, or something that overpowered thought. All I can tell is, it seemed to me that either I had never loved England, or I had loved it foolishly, æsthetically, like a slave, not having realized that it was not mine unless I were willing and prepared to die rather than leave it as Belgian women and old men and children had left their country. Something I had omitted. Something, I felt, had to be done before I could look again composedly at English landscape, at the elms and poplars about the houses, at the purple-headed wood-betony with two pairs of dark leaves on a stiff stem, who stood sentinel among the grasses or bracken by hedge-side or wood's-edge. What he stood sentinel for I did not know, any more than what I had got to do.

The Last Sheaf

The sun used to shine

The sun used to shine while we two walked
Slowly together, paused and started
Again, and sometimes mused, sometimes talked
As either pleased, and cheerfully parted

Each night. We never disagreed
Which gate to rest on. The to be
And the late past we gave small heed.
We turned from men or poetry

To rumours of the war remote
Only till both stood disinclined
For aught but the yellow flavorous coat
Of an apple wasps had undermined;

Or a sentry of dark betonies,
The stateliest of small flowers on earth,
At the forest verge; or crocuses
Pale purple as if they had their birth

In sunless Hades fields. The war
Came back to mind with the moonrise
Which soldiers in the east afar
Beheld then. Nevertheless, our eyes

Could as well imagine the Crusades
Or Caesar's battles. Everything
To faintness like those rumours fades—
Like the brook's water glittering

Under the moonlight—like those walks
Now—like us two that took them, and
The fallen apples, all the talks
And silences—like memory's sand

When the tide covers it late or soon,
And other men through other flowers
In those fields under the same moon
Go talking and have easy hours.

February Afternoon

Men heard this roar of parleying starlings, saw,
A thousand years ago even as now,
Black rooks with white gulls following the plough
So that the first are last until a caw
Commands that last are first again,— a law
Which was of old when one, like me, dreamed how
A thousand years might dust lie on his brow
Yet thus would birds do between hedge and shaw.

Time swims before me, making as a day
A thousand years, while the broad ploughland oak
Roars mill-like and men strike and bear the stroke
Of war as ever, audacious or resigned,
And God still sits aloft in the array
That we have wrought him, stone-deaf and stone-blind.

May 23

There never was a finer day,
And never will be while May is May,—

The third, and not the last of its kind;
But though fair and clear the two behind
Seemed pursued by tempests overpast;
And the morrow with fear that it could not last
Was spoiled. Today ere the stones were warm
Five minutes of thunderstorm
Dashed it with rain, as if to secure,
By one tear, its beauty the luck to endure.

At midday then along the lane
Old Jack Noman appeared again,
Jaunty and old, crooked and tall,
And stopped and grinned at me over the wall,
With a cowslip bunch in his button-hole
And one in his cap. Who could say if his roll

Came from flints in the road, the weather, or ale?
He was welcome as the nightingale.
Not an hour of the sun had been wasted on Jack.

'I've got my Indian complexion back'
Said he. He was tanned like a harvester,–
Like his short clay pipe, like the leaf and bur–
That clung to his coat from last night's bed,
Like the ploughland crumbling red.
Fairer flowers were none on the earth
Than his cowslips wet with the dew of their birth,
Or fresher leaves than the cress in his basket.
'Where did they come from, Jack?' 'Don't ask it,
And you'll be told no lies.' 'Very well:
Then I can't buy.' 'I don't want to sell.
Take them and these flowers, too, free.
Perhaps you have something to give me?

Wait till next time. The better the day…
The Lord couldn't make a better, I say;
If he could, he never has done'.
So off went Jack with his roll-walk-run,
Leaving his cresses from Oakshott rill
And his cowslips from Wheatham hill.

'Twas the first day that the midges bit;
But though they bit me, I was glad of it:
Of the dust in my face, too, I was glad.
Spring could do nothing to make me sad.
Bluebells hid all the ruts in the copse.
The elm seeds lay in the road like hops,
That fine day, May the twenty-third,
The day Jack Noman disappeared.

The Green Roads

The green roads that end in the forest
Are strewn with white goose feathers this June,

Like marks left behind by some one gone to the forest
To show his track. But he has never come back.

Down each green road a cottage looks at the forest.
Round one the nettle towers; two are bathed in flowers.

An old man along the green road to the forest
Strays from one, from another a child alone.

In the thicket bordering the forest,
All day long a thrush twiddles his song.

It is old, but the trees are young in the forest,
All but one like a castle keep, in the middle deep.

That oak saw the ages pass in the forest:
They were a host, but their memories are lost,

For the tree is dead: all things forget the forest
Excepting perhaps me, when now I see

The old man, the child, the goose feathers at the edge
  of the forest,
And hear all day long the thrush repeat his song.

The Brook

Seated once by a brook, watching a child
Chiefly that paddled, I was thus beguiled.
Mellow the blackbird sang and sharp the thrush
Not far off in the oak and hazel brush,
Unseen. There was a scent like honeycomb
From mugwort dull. And down upon the dome
Of the stone the cart-horse kicks against so oft
A butterfly alighted. From aloft
He took the heat of the sun, and from below.
On the hot stone he perched contented so,
As if never a cart would pass again
That way; as if I were the last of men
And he the first of insects to have earth
And sun together and to know their worth.

I was divided between him and the gleam,
The motion, and the voices, of the stream,
The waters running frizzled over gravel,
That never vanish and for ever travel.
A grey flycatcher silent on a fence
And I sat as if we had been there since
The horseman and the horse lying beneath
The fir-tree-covered barrow on the heath,
The horseman and the horse with silver shoes,
Galloped the downs last. All that I could lose
I lost. And then the child's voice raised the dead.
'No one's been here before' was what she said
And what I felt, yet never should have found
A word for, while I gathered sight and sound.

As the team's head brass

As the team's head brass flashed out on the turn
The lovers disappeared into the wood.
I sat among the boughs of the fallen elm
That strewed an angle of the fallow, and
Watched the plough narrowing a yellow square
Of charlock. Every time the horses turned
Instead of treading me down, the ploughman leaned
Upon the handles to say or ask a word,
About the weather, next about the war.
Scraping the share he faced towards the wood,
And screwed along the furrow till the brass flashed
Once more.

The blizzard felled the elm whose crest
I sat in, by a woodpecker's round hole,
The ploughman said. 'When will they take it away?'
'When the war's over.' So the talk began—
One minute and an interval of ten,
A minute more and the same interval.

'Have you been out?' 'No.' 'And don't want to, perhaps?'
'If I could only come back again, I should.
I could spare an arm. I shouldn't want to lose
A leg. If I should lose my head, why, so,
I should want nothing more.... Have many gone
From here?' 'Yes.' 'Many lost?' 'Yes, a good few.
Only two teams work on the farm this year.
One of my mates is dead. The second day
In France they killed him. It was back in March,
The very night of the blizzard, too. Now if
He had stayed here we should have moved the tree.'
'And I should not have sat here. Everything
Would have been different. For it would have been
Another world.' 'Ay, and a better, though
If we could see all all might seem good.' Then
The lovers came out of the wood again:
The horses started and for the last time
I watched the clods crumble and topple over
After the ploughshare and the stumbling team.

Wind and Mist

They met inside the gateway that gives the view,
A hollow land as vast as heaven. 'It is
A pleasant day, sir.' 'A very pleasant day.'
'And what a view here. If you like angled fields
Of grass and grain bounded by oak and thorn,
Here is a league. Had we with Germany
To play upon this board it could not be
More dear than April has made it with a smile.
The fields beyond that league close in together
And merge, even as our days into the past,
Into one wood that has a shining pane
Of water. Then the hills of the horizon—
That is how I should make hills had I to show
One who would never see them what hills were like.'
'Yes. Sixty miles of South Downs at one glance.
Sometimes a man feels proud at them, as if
He had just created them with one mighty thought.'

'That house, though modern, could not better planned
For its position. I never liked a new
House better. Could you tell me who lives in it?'
'No one'. Ah–and I was peopling all
Those windows on the south with happy eyes,
The terrace under them with happy feet;
Girls–' 'Sir, I know. I know. I have seen that house
Through mist look lovely as a castle in Spain,
And airier. I have thought: "'Twere happy there
To live." And I have laughed at that
Because I lived there then'. Extraordinary.'
'Yes, with my furniture and family
Still in it, I, knowing every nook of it
And loving none, and in fact hating it.'
'Dear me! How could that be? But pardon me.'
'No offence. Doubtless the house was not to blame,
But the eye watching from those windows saw,
Many a day, day after day, mist–mist
Like chaos surging back–and felt itself
Alone in all the world, marooned alone.

We lived in clouds, on a cliff's edge almost
(You see), and if clouds went, the visible earth
Lay too far off beneath and like a cloud.
I did not know it was the earth I loved
Until I tried to live there in the clouds
And the earth turned to cloud.'

'You had a garden
Of flint and clay, too.' 'True; that was real enough.
The flint was the one crop that never failed.
The clay first broke my heart, and then my back;
And the back heals not. There were other things
Real, too. In that room at the gable a child
Was born while the wind chilled a summer dawn:
Never looked grey mind on a greyer one
Than when the child's cry broke above the groans.'
'I hope they were both spared.' 'They were. Oh yes.
But flint and clay and childbirth were too real
For this cloud castle. I had forgot the wind.
Pray do not let me get on to the wind.
You would not understand about the wind.

It is my subject, and compared with me
Those who have always lived on the firm ground
Are quite unreal in this matter of the wind.
There were whole days and nights when the wind and I
Between us shared the world, and the wind ruled
And I obeyed it and forgot the mist.
My past and the past of the world were in the wind.

Now you will say that though you understand
And feel for me, and so on, you yourself
Would find it different. You are all like that
If once you stand here free from wind and mist:
I might as well be talking to wind and mist.
You would believe the house-agent's young man
Who gives no heed to anything I say.
Good morning. But one word. I want to admit
That I would try the house once more, if I could;
As I should like to try being young again.'

Blenheim Oranges

Gone, gone again,
May, June, July,
And August gone,
Again gone by,

Not memorable
Save that I saw them go,
As past the empty quays
The rivers flow.

And now again,
In the harvest rain,
The Blenheim oranges
Fall grubby from the trees,

As when I was young–
And when the lost one was here–
And when the war began
To turn young men to dung.

Look at the old house,
Outmoded, dignified,
Dark and untenanted,
With grass growing instead

Of the footsteps of life,
The friendliness, the strife;
In its beds have lain
Youth, love, age and pain:

I am something like that;
Only I am not dead,
Still breathing and interested
In the house that is not dark:—

I am something like that:
Not one pane to reflect the sun,
For the schoolboys to throw at—
They have broken every one.

Parting

The Past is a strange land, most strange.
Wind blows not there, nor does rain fall:
If they do, they cannot hurt at all.
Men of all kinds as equals range

The soundless fields and streets of it.
Pleasure and pain there have no sting,
The perished self not suffering
That lacks all blood and nerve and wit,

And is in shadow-land a shade.
Remembered joy and misery
Bring joy to the joyous equally;
Both sadden the sad. So memory made

Parting today a double pain:
First because it was parting; next
Because the ill it ended vexed
And mocked me from the Past again,

Not as what had been remedied
Had I gone on,– not that, oh no!
But as itself no longer woe;
Sighs, angry word and look and deed

Being faded: rather a kind of bliss,
For there spiritualized it lay
In the perpetual yesterday
That naught can stir or stain, like this.

Tears

It seems I have no tears left. They should have fallen–
Their ghosts, if tears have ghosts, did fall–that day
When twenty hounds streamed by me, not yet combed out
But still all equals in their rage of gladness
Upon the scent, made one, like a great dragon
In Blooming Meadow that bends towards the sun
And once bore hops: and on that other day
When I stepped out from the double-shadowed Tower
Into an April morning, stirring and sweet
And warm. Strange solitude was there and silence.
A mightier charm than any in the Tower
Possessed the courtyard. They were changing guard,
Soldiers in line, young English countrymen,
Fair-haired and ruddy, in white tunics. Drums
And fifes were playing 'The British Grenadiers.'
The men, the music piercing that solitude
And silence, told me truths I had not dreamed,
And have forgotten since their beauty passed.

Cock-Crow

Out of the wood of thoughts that grows by night
To be cut down by the sharp axe of light,–
Out of the night, two cocks together crow,
Cleaving the darkness with a silver blow:
And bright before my eyes twin trumpeters stand,
Heralds of splendour, one at either hand,
Each facing each as in a coat of arms:
The milkers lace their boots up at the farms.

In Memoriam

The flowers left thick at nightfall in the wood
This Eastertide call into mind the men,
Now far from home, who, with their sweethearts, should
Have gathered them and will do never again.

Easter, 1915

The Cherry Trees

The cherry trees bend over and are shedding
On the old road where all that passed are dead
Their petals, strewing the grass as for a wedding
This early May morn when there is none to wed.

Fifty Faggots

There they stand, on their ends, the fifty faggots
That once were underwood of hazel and ash
In Jenny Pinks's Copse. Now, by the hedge
Close packed, they make a thicket fancy alone
Can creep through with the mouse and wren. Next Spring
A blackbird or a robin will nest there,
Accustomed to them, thinking they will remain
Whatever is for ever to a bird:
This Spring it is too late; the swift has come.
'Twas a hot day for carrying them up:
Better they will never warm me, though they must
Light several Winters' fires. Before they are done
The war will have ended, many other things
Have ended, maybe, that I can no more
Foresee or more control than robin and wren.

Digging 2

What matter makes my spade for tears or mirth,
Letting down two clay pipes into the earth?
The one I smoked, the other a soldier
Of Blenheim, Ramillies, and Malplaquet
Perhaps. The dead man's immortality
Lies represented lightly with my own,
A yard or two nearer the living air
Than bones of ancients who, amazed to see
Almighty God erect the mastodon,
Once laughed, or wept, in this same light of day.

Song

Early one morning in May I set out,
And nobody I knew was about.
I'm bound away for ever,
Away somewhere, away for ever.

There was no wind to trouble the weathercocks.
I had burnt my letters and darned my socks.

No one knew I was going away,
I thought myself I should come back some day.

I heard the brook through the town gardens run.
O sweet was the mud turned to dust by the sun.

A gate banged in a fence and banged in my head.
'A fine morning, sir,' a shepherd said.

I could not return from my liberty,
To my youth and my love and my misery.

The past is the only dead thing that smells sweet,
The only sweet thing that is not also fleet.
I'm bound away for ever,
Away somewhere, away for ever.

There was a time

There was a time when this poor frame was whole
And I had youth and never another care,
Or none that should have troubled a strong soul.
Yet, except sometimes in a frosty air
When my heels hammered out a melody
From pavements of a city left behind,
I never would acknowledge my own glee
Because it was less mighty than my mind
Had dreamed of. Since I could not boast of strength
Great as I wished, weakness was all my boast.
I sought yet hated pity till at length
I earned it. Oh, too heavy was the cost.
But now that there is something I could use
My youth and strength for, I deny the age,
The care and weakness that I know—refuse
To admit I am unworthy of the wage
Paid to a man who gives up eyes and breath
For what can neither ask nor heed his death.

When first

When first I came here I had hope,
Hope for I knew not what. Fast beat
My heart at sight of the tall slope
Of grass and yews, as if my feet

Only by scaling its steps of chalk
Would see something no other hill
Ever disclosed. And now I walk
Down it the last time. Never will

My heart beat so again at sight
Of any hill although as fair
And loftier. For infinite
The change, late unperceived, this year,

The twelfth, suddenly, shows me plain.
Hope now,—not health, nor cheerfulness,
Since they can come and go again,
As often one brief hour witnesses,—

Just hope has gone for ever. Perhaps
I may love other hills yet more
Than this: the future and the maps
Hide something I was waiting for.

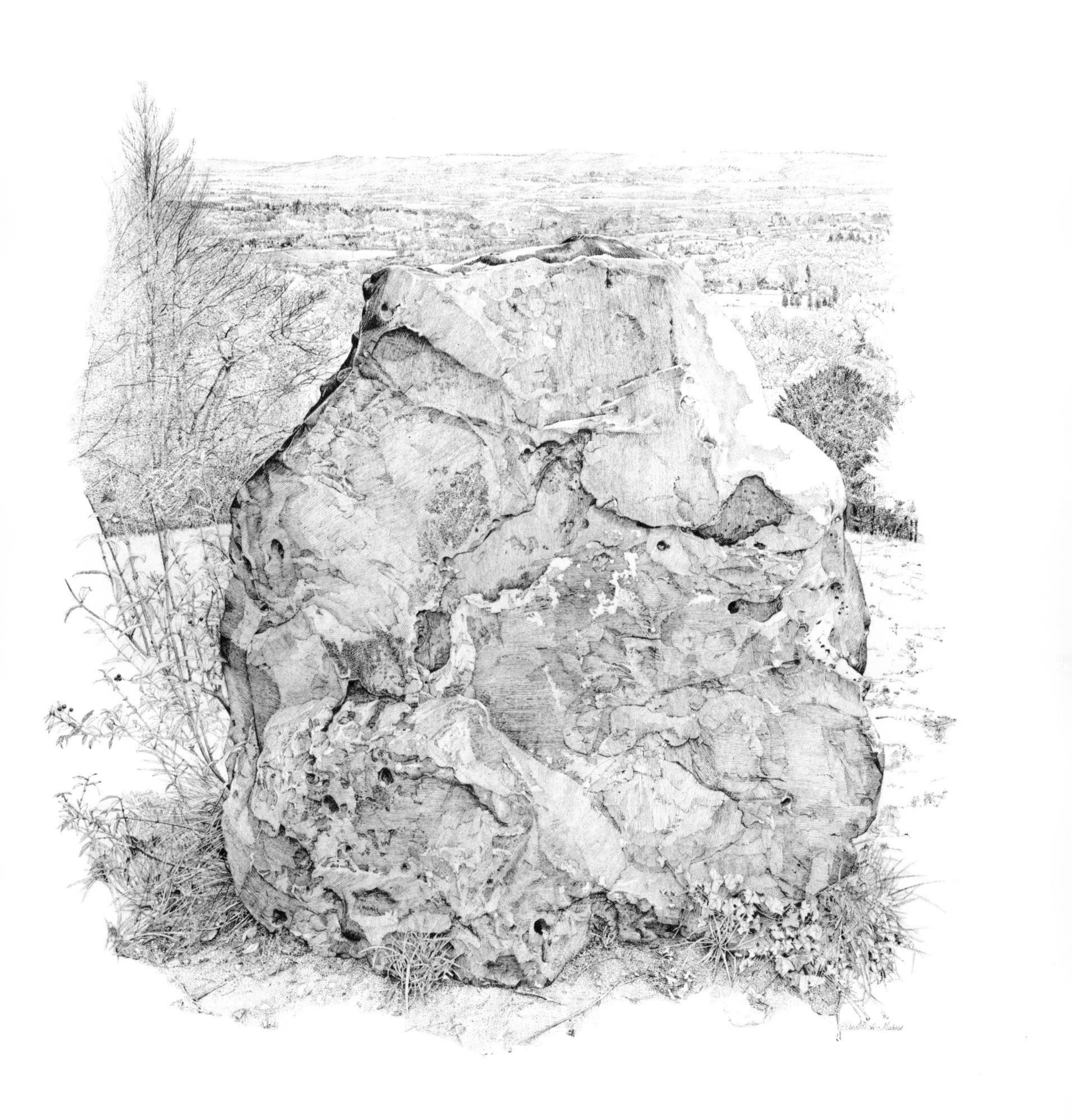

Over the Hills

Often and often it came back again
To mind, the day I passed the horizon ridge
To a new country, the path I had to find
By half-gaps that were stiles once in the hedge,
The pack of scarlet clouds running across
The harvest evening that seemed endless then
And after, and the inn where all were kind,
All were strangers. I did not know my loss
Till one day twelve months later suddenly
I leaned upon my spade and saw it all,
Though far beyond the sky-line. It became
Almost a habit through the year for me
To lean and see it and think to do the same
Again for two days and a night. Recall
Was vain: no more could the restless brook
Ever turn back and climb the waterfall
To the lake that rests and stirs not in its nook,
As in the hollow of the collar-bone
Under the mountain's head of rush and stone.

What will they do?

What will they do when I am gone? It is plain
That they will do without me as the rain
Can do without the flowers and the grass
That profit by it and must perish without.
I have but seen them in the loud street pass;
And I was naught to them. I turned about
To see them disappearing carelessly.
But what if I in them as they in me
Nourished what has great value and no price?
Almost I thought that rain thirsts for a draught
Which only in the blossom's chalice lies,
Until that one turned back and lightly laughed.

Roads

I love roads:
The goddesses that dwell
Far along invisible
Are my favourite gods.

Roads go on
While we forget, and are
Forgotten like a star~
That shoots and is gone.

On this earth 'tis sure
We men have not made
Anything that doth fade
So soon, so long endure:

The hill road wet with rain
In the sun would not gleam
Like a winding stream
If we trod it not again.

They are lonely
While we sleep, lonelier
For lack of the traveller
Who is now a dream only.

From dawn's twilight
And all the clouds like sheep
On the mountains of sleep
They wind into the night.

The next turn may reveal
Heaven: upon the crest
The close pine clump, at rest
And black, may Hell conceal.

Often footsore, never
Yet of the road I weary,
Though long and steep and dreary
As it winds on for ever.

Helen of the roads,
The mountain ways of Wales
And the Mabinogion tales,
Is one of the true gods,

Abiding in the trees,
The threes and fours so wise,
The larger companies,
That by the roadside be,

And beneath the rafter
Else uninhabited
Excepting by the dead;
And it is her laughter

At morn and night I hear
When the thrush cock sings
Bright irrelevant things,
And when the chanticleer

Calls back to their own night
Troops that make loneliness
With their light footsteps' press,
As Helen's own are light.

Now all roads lead to France
And heavy is the tread
Of the living; but the dead
Returning lightly dance:

Whatever the road bring
To me or take from me,
They keep me company
With their pattering,

Crowding the solitude
Of the loops over the downs,
Hushing the roar of towns
And their brief multitude.

'Home' 3

Fair was the morning, fair our tempers, and
We had seen nothing fairer than that land,

Though strange, and the untrodden snow that made
Wild of the tame, casting out all that was
Not wild and rustic and old; and we were glad.

Fair too was afternoon, and first to pass
Were we that league of snow, next the north wind.

There was nothing to return for except need.
And yet we sang nor ever stopped for speed,
As we did often with the start behind.
Faster still strode we when we came in sight
Of the cold roofs where we must spend the night.

Happy we had not been there, nor could be,
Though we had tasted sleep and food and fellowship
Together long.
'How quick' to someone's lip
The word came, 'will the beaten horse run home'.

The word 'home' raised a smile in us all three,
And one repeated it, smiling just so
That all knew what he meant and none would say.
Between three counties far apart that lay
We were divided and looked strangely each
At the other, and we knew we were not friends
But fellows in a union that ends
With the necessity for it, as it ought.

Never a word was spoken, not a thought
Was thought, of what the look meant with the word
'Home' as we walked and watched the sunset blurred.
And then to me the word, only the word,
'Homesick', as it were playfully occurred:
No more. If I should ever more admit
Than the mere word I could not endure it
For a day longer: this captivity
Must somehow come to an end, else I should be
Another man, as often now I seem,
Or this life be only an evil dream.

The Trumpet

Rise up, rise up,
And, as the trumpet blowing
Chases the dreams of men,
As the dawn glowing
The stars that left unlit
The land and water,
Rise up and scatter
The dew that covers
The print of last night's lovers—
Scatter it, scatter it!

While you are listening
To the clear horn,
Forget, men, everything
On this earth newborn,
Except that it is lovelier
Than any mysteries.
Open your eyes to the air
That has washed the eyes of the stars
Through all the dewy night:
Up with the light,
To the old wars;
Arise, arise!

Bugle Call

'No one cares less than I,
Nobody knows but God,
Whether I am destined to lie
Under a foreign clod'
Were the words I made to the bugle call in the morning.

But laughing, storming, scorning,
Only the bugles know
What the bugles say in the morning,
And they do not care, when they blow
The call that I heard and made words to early this morning.

A Private

This ploughman dead in battle slept out of doors
Many a frosty night, and merrily
Answered staid drinkers, good bedmen, and all bores:
'At Mrs Greenland's Hawthorn Bush', said he,
'I slept'. None knew which bush. Above the town,
Beyond 'The Drover', a hundred spot the down
In Wiltshire. And where now at last he sleeps
More sound in France — that, too, he secret keeps.

The Owl

Downhill I came, hungry, and yet not starved;
Cold, yet had heat within me that was proof
Against the North wind; tired, yet so that rest
Had seemed the sweetest thing under a roof.

Then at the inn I had food, fire, and rest,
Knowing how hungry, cold, and tired was I.
All of the night was quite barred out except
An owl's cry, a most melancholy cry

Shaken out long and clear upon the hill,
No merry note, nor cause of merriment,
But one telling me plain what I escaped
And others could not, that night, as in I went.

And salted was my food, and my repose,
Salted and sobered, too, by the bird's voice
Speaking for all who lay under the stars,
Soldiers and poor, unable to rejoice.

Home 1

Not the end: but there's nothing more.
Sweet Summer and Winter rude
I have loved, and friendship and love,
The crowd and solitude:

But I know them: I weary not;
But all that they mean I know.
I would go back again home
Now. Yet how should I go?

This is my grief. That land,
My home, I have never seen;
No traveller tells of it,
However far he has been.

And could I discover it,
I fear my happiness there,
Or my pain, might be dreams of return
Here, to these things that were.

Remembering ills, though slight
Yet irremediable,
Brings a worse, an impurer pang
Than remembering what was well.

No: I cannot go back,
And would not if I could.
Until blindness come, I must wait
And blink at what is not good.

Out in the dark

Out in the dark over the snow
The fallow fawns invisible go
With the fallow doe;
And the winds blow
Fast as the stars are slow.

Stealthily the dark haunts round
And, when a lamp goes, without sound
At a swifter bound
Than the swiftest hound,
Arrives, and all else is drowned;

And I and star and wind and deer
Are in the dark together,—near,
Yet far,—and fear
Drums on my ear
In that sage company drear.

How weak and little is the light,
All the universe of sight,
Love and delight,
Before the might,
If you love it not, of night.

Rain

Rain, midnight rain, nothing but the wild rain
On this bleak hut, and solitude, and me
Remembering again that I shall die
And neither hear the rain nor give it thanks
For washing me cleaner than I have been
Since I was born into this solitude.
Blessed are the dead that the rain rains upon:
But here I pray that none whom once I loved
Is dying tonight or lying still awake
Solitary, listening to the rain,
Either in pain or thus in sympathy
Helpless among the living and the dead,
Like a cold water among broken reeds,
Myriads of broken reeds all still and stiff,
Like me who have no love which this wild rain
Has not dissolved except the love of death,
If love it be towards what is perfect and
Cannot, the tempest tells me, disappoint.

Liberty

The last light has gone out of the world, except
This moonlight lying on the grass like frost
Beyond the brink of the tall elm's shadow.
It is as if everything else had slept
Many an age, unforgotten and lost
The men that were, the things done, long ago,
All I have thought; and but the moon and I
Live yet and here stand idle over the grave
Where all is buried. Both have liberty
To dream what we could do if we were free
To do some thing we had desired long,
The moon and I. There's none less free than who
Does nothing and has nothing else to do,
Being free only for what is not to his mind,

And nothing is to his mind. If every hour
Like this one passing that I have spent among
The wiser others when I have forgot
To wonder whether I was free or not,
Were piled before me, and not lost behind,
And I could take and carry them away
I should be rich; or if I had the power
To wipe out every one and not again
Regret, I should be rich to be so poor.
And yet I still am half in love with pain,
With what is imperfect, with both tears and mirth,
With things that have an end, with life and earth,
And this moon that leaves me dark within the door.

Lights Out

I have come to the borders of sleep,
The unfathomable deep
Forest, where all must lose
Their way, however straight
Or winding, soon or late;
They can not choose.

Many a road and track
That since the dawn's first crack
Up to the forest brink
Deceived the travellers,
Suddenly now blurs,
And in they sink.

Here love ends—
Despair, ambition ends;

All pleasure and all trouble,
Although most sweet or bitter,
Here ends, in sleep that is sweeter
Than tasks most noble.

There is not any book
Or face of dearest look
That I would not turn from now
To go into the unknown
I must enter, and leave, alone,
I know not how.

The tall forest towers:
Its cloudy foliage lowers
Ahead, shelf above shelf:
Its silence I hear and obey
That I may lose my way
And myself.

Last Poem

The sorrow of true love is a great sorrow
And true love parting blackens a bright morrow:
Yet almost they equal joys, since their despair
Is but hope blinded by its tears, and clear
Above the storm the heavens wait to be seen.
But greater sorrow from less love has been
That can mistake lack of despair for hope
And knows not tempest and the perfect scope
Of summer, but a frozen drizzle perpetual
Of drops that from remorse and pity fall
And cannot ever shine in the sun or thaw,
Removed eternally from the sun's law.

13.1.17.

Finis